VINTAGE ROADSCENE SPECIAL

First published 1985

ISBN 0 7110 1563 5

Published by Ian Allan Ltd, Shepperton, Surrey; and printed by Ian Allan Printing Ltd at their works at Coombelands in Runnymede, England

Cover:
London County Council tramcar No 106, preserved at the National Tramway Museum, Crich.
Peter Johnson

Below:
A scene at the National Tramway Museum, Crich. Glasgow No 812 passing London County Council No 106 in the summer of 1984 at the Wakebridge Crossing place. On the right is Glasgow works car No 21 which was once used as the museum bookshop. The extension to Glory Mine can be seen between the operating cars. *Author*

BRITISH TRAMS & TRAMWAYS in the 1980s

Contents

BRITISH TRAMS & TRAMWAYS in the 1980s

Introduction

Speak to many people about British trams and tramways and most will regret their passing, labouring under the misapprehension that the classic British street tramway is a part of history. And so it is in most towns and cities. Yet even in the 1980s it is possible to ride through public streets on tramcars both ancient and modern, in Blackpool, Douglas, Isle of Man and Fleetwood.

This mileage is quite small, it must be said, but there is, by comparison, a considerable additional mileage operated on reserved track. The majority of the tramways between Blackpool and

Fleetwood and Douglas and Ramsey are of this type, as is the Seaton Tramway which was mainly built on the formation of an ex-BR branch line. The Great Orme Tramway is also mainly reserved track, the small section of street track being closed to motor vehicles during the hours of tramway operation.

The old tramway undertakings showed even less inclination to preserve relics of their past than the contemporary railway companies. Equally museum curators did not consider public transport to be part of their remit; the only exception was at Hull, where the Ryde Pier horse car and the

Portstewart tram engine were displayed in the road transport gallery, but these were not 'collected' by the Museum and it is only now that a Hull tramcar is being prepared for addition to the exhibition. By 1939 only four cars had been officially put aside, for preservation, by their owners; there were apparently no plans to display them to the public.

After the last war there was an increasing awareness of the value of conservation, both publicly and privately; it is this, and the increase in available leisure time, which is responsible for the 100 plus tramcars which have been collected since. Many of these vehicles are still awaiting either restoration or public display but a good number are accessible to the public, many in working order.

When enthusiasts started collecting trams, from 1948, they wanted to be able to house them where they could be operated, following the example of the pioneer railway preservationists. The National Tramway Museum at Crich, opened in 1959, proved to be the forerunner of working museum lines at Beamish, Carlton Colville, Dudley and Manchester. A feature of these museum lines, when compared with comparable railway ventures, is their short length. The longest, at Crich, is only just over a mile long; this cannot be a drawback for it appears to provide a demonstration tramride acceptable to both operators and passengers alike. There are plans for extensions but these are more likely to be considered in terms of hundreds of yards, rather than

Left:
Paisley District No 68 was built as an open-top car in 1919. Four years later the Paisley system was absorbed by Glasgow Corporation which eventually resulted in No 68 becoming totally enclosed. Acquired for preservation in 1954, it arrived at Crich in 1960. Restored to Paisley condition No 68 was decorated for the Royal Wedding in 1981 and, as shown here, for the museum's 25th anniversary in 1984. *Author*

Left:
Travelling tram. Liverpool No 869 was built in 1936, sold to Glasgow in 1953 and was preserved in 1960. It arrived at Crich in 1961, only to leave again in 1967 when it was decided to restore the car in Liverpool itself. It is shown on display at the Merseyside PTE's Edge Lane works open day on 29 September 1979, just before it was returned to Crich. *M. F. Haddon*

increasing number of British planners are finding light rapid transit, the modern tramway, an attractive solution to traffic congestion; already schemes incorporating street running are being proposed for Birmingham and Manchester. If they should come to fruition the future of the British tramway will most certainly be assured.

Acknowledgements
I am particularly indebted to Mike Haddon for supplying so many fine photographs for use herein. They have enabled the coverage to be so much wider than would have been possible without them.

The bibliography used in this work has been quite extensive, regrettably space does not permit a full listing. I would, however, like to draw attention to the following, which were of great value.

Abell, P.H.; *British Tramway Guide*; Author, 1984.

Anderson, R.C.; *Great Orme Tramway the first 80 years*; Light Rail Transit Association, 1982.

Higgs, Philip; *Blackpool's Trams 'as popular as the Tower'*; Lancastrian Transport Group, 1984.

Joyce, J.; *Vintage Roadscene Special – Blackpool's Trams;* Ian Allan, 1985.

Mackenzie, Jeffrey; *Always a Tram in Sight: A picture history of Blackpool's trams*; Light Railway Transport League, 1972.

Palmer, G.S.; *By tram to the Tower*; Author, 1965.

Palmer, G.S. & Turner, B.R.; *Blackpool by Tram*; Authors, 1968, 1978, 1981.

Palmer, G.S. & Turner, B.R.; *Trams and Buses around Blackpool*; Authors, 1982.

Palmer, Steve; *Blackpool's Century of Trams*; Blackpool Corporation Transport, 1985.

Pearson, F.K.; *Isle of Man Tramways*; David & Charles, 1970.

Price, J.H.; *The Seaton Tramway*; Light Railway Transport League, 1974.

Turner, Brian; *Blackpool to Fleetwood*; Light Railway Transport League, 1977.

Other sources included the Tramway Museum Society's quarterly *Journal* and the Light Rail Transit Association's monthly *Modern Tramway* (published jointly with Ian Allan Ltd).

Given more room, several peripheral topics would have been included. The Shipley Glen tramway, 90 years old in 1985, the Volk's Electric Railway and the miner's tramway at Llechwedd Slate Caverns in Blaenau Ffestiniog are all worthy of further study and attention.

Peter Johnson
Leicester

miles. Whereas local authorities have not involved themselves in private railway operation, although some have provided capital support for schemes in their areas, this has not been the case when it comes to tramway creation; the lines at Beamish and Dudley are both part of much larger ventures, open air museums, where a tramway is seen to be an ideal way of transporting visitors about the site, providing an experience in its own right. The Spen Valley tramway, being promoted by West Yorkshire Metropolitan County Council, promises to be a much larger undertaking than those already mentioned.

Many of those concerned with tramway operation in museum conditions are as concerned about the backcloth in front of which their cars run as they are with the appearance of the cars themselves. As a result a number of fine street scenes are being developed using suitable buildings, often being threatened with demolition from elsewhere. The authentic scenes thus created are often only spoiled by the modern appearance of the visitors!

The museum cars have come from a number of sources. A few were bought from, or donated by, undertakings closing down in the 1950s – the last closure, at Glasgow, took place in 1962. Many of these cars were comparatively modern; some much older cars had survived in works fleets and have been restored to original condition. Many operators sold unwanted tram bodies for further use – holiday chalets, chicken sheds and sports pavilions, for example. They have been found in varying degrees of completeness but already some very fine restorations have taken place. (Tramcar restoration is a very expensive business – the recent overhaul of Blackpool 40, at Crich, cost £40,000 and it was a complete vehicle to start with). A trend which is likely to continue is the importation of cars from abroad. Foreign trams add to an existing collection; they are likely to form the mainstay of any new operating lines. Operators overseas have proved to be a useful source of major spares, such as trucks and controllers, needed for many restorations.

The first British electric tramway was opened in Blackpool in 1885. In a modified form this original line continues in daily use. One hundred years ago Blackpool was being very innovative. The innovations continue with modern tramcars entering traffic in the 1980s, the investment for them being very hard won. The prototype single-deck cars now being evaluated are obviously derived from British experience and outwardly show no evidence of development elsewhere, although that is not the case with some of the mechanical components. Tramways have never lost favour on the Continent and are under constant development. Continental practices have been incorporated into the Tyne & Wear Metro. Although the Metrocars have yet to take to the streets, this could change if proposed extensions are ever built. More development on these lines are likely to be incorporated into the London Docklands Light Railway now under construction. Elsewhere an

Blackpool Corporation Tramway

The 11½-mile tram route remaining in Blackpool is an amalgamation of the coastal routes of two operators, Blackpool Corporation and the Blackpool & Fleetwood Tramroad Company.

The first electric tramway in Blackpool was opened on 29 September 1885. The service was operated by the Blackpool Electric Tramways Co on a route which ran along the Promenade, between Cocker Street and South Pier, just short of two miles long. The actual tramway was owned by the council which leased it to the company. A depot was built in Blundell Street, with access via Foxhall Square and Princess Street; the depot survived until the 1980s when it was demolished, but the route along Princess Street remains, the only section of the original tramway to survive in the same location; it is not used regularly as it is an alternative route to the Rigby Road depot. (The main line of tramway was moved from the highway onto a reserved section of the widened Promenade which was opened in 1905). The track was mostly single; there were 10 passing places and a short section of double track, a third of a mile long, at Central Beach.

The tramway just described was the first electric street tramway in the British Isles. In consequence there was no precedent to draw upon when it came to deciding upon the means of supplying electricity to the cars. It is perhaps not surprising that a conduit system was chosen, as this put the power out of harm's way, under the road surface; it also avoided the need to erect poles, often considered unsightly by the Victorians, for an overhead system. A similar conduit system was used successfully in central London for many years but the seaside was not an ideal location for it, as the operators found to their cost. The ease with which the egress of sand and sea water into the conduit caused disruption to the services was the reason for its abandonment. Overhead was erected and brought into use on 13 June 1899.

The first tram fleet consisted of 10 cars. There were six closed cars, suitable for year-round use, and four open cars for the summer. Two open trailer cars were single-deck vehicles, whilst the remainder were double-deckers. The trailers were introduced without prior approval and were rapidly withdrawn following objections from the Blackpool Carriage Proprietors' Association which were upheld by the council. Many years later they were modified and ended their careers as . . . cabmen's shelters!

By the time the overhead replaced the conduit in 1899, the tramway had been operated by the council for seven years. The company had withdrawn when its lease expired and new operators had not come forward. The whole undertaking was badly run down and probably gave the council, which put in an inexperienced management team, even more problems than it did the company. Continuing difficulties with the conduit were overcome by the simple expedient of switching off the power! Horses were substituted for electricity until the overhead was erected.

The first tramway extension was opened in 1895. The new route followd the Lytham Road to Squires Gate passing Waterloo Road (now Blackpool South) station en route. At this stage the council had not decided how to resolve the problematic conduit on the Promenade, yet it had to act before its powers to build lapsed. A compromise was reached; part was electrified, using the conduit, and part was horse-powered – the station was the changeover point. Two years later a link line to the Promenade was put in along Station Road; it was equipped with the last conduit track laid in Blackpool. Being further from the front these sections of conduit were reasonably effective but

Right:
Blackpool at the Tower on 19 September 1981. A typical Blackpool scene with people and trams wherever you look. In addition to the 'Balloon' disappearing into the distance there is – at left – a one-man car heading northwards; a twinset terminating, centre; and No 761, the first of the 'Balloon' rebuilds, bound for the Pleasure Beach on the right. There are boards advertising the special cars' tours of the illuminations propped against the shelter on the left. *M. F. Haddon*

continuing difficulties with it only emphasised the need for an improved method of current collection.

The first years of the 20th century saw the system expanded almost to its greatest extent. The Promenade route was extended northwards to Gynn Square in 1900. At the same time the northern section of the original line was doubled. The following year the Marton line was opened with the objective of opening up the back of the town, then extremely rural, to development. The route was almost circular, being connected to the Promenade line at both Talbot Square and Central station. The line came into its own with both the interwar housing development and the introduction of the famous circular tours. In 1902 a link to the Lytham Road route at the Royal Oak was opened. This also served Waterloo Road station. The final extension at this time was to Layton, also opened in 1902; it was expected that most revenue would be generated by visitors to the municipal cemetery. It also served Talbot Road (now called Blackpool North) station and was connected to the Promenade route at Talbot Square.

The two 1885-built open trailers, rejected by the council, were replaced by two enclosed cars in 1891; they were the last vehicles put into service by the company. In each of the years of 1894, 1896 and 1898, the council added two more cars to the fleet. The 1894 and 1896 additions were, by the standards of the day, massive vehicles capable of seating 82 passengers. They were a step in the right direction, for an ever increasing number were riding on the town's trams, but they were cumbersome in loading, taking seven minutes at peak times. The 1898 cars, the last built for the conduit, were to show the way forward. (All the cars mentioned here, and the remaining eight 1885 cars, were converted to overhead current collection in 1899).

Seating 86 passengers, 36 inside and 50 upstairs, in the open, the 1898 cars were ideal for Blackpool, notably because the twin staircases at either end made for rapid loading and unloading. Further deliveries were made in 1900 (10) and 1902 (8). As they proceeded sedately along the Promenade they must have presented an awesome sight to the Edwardian holiday makers; it is hardly surprising that the launching of HMS *Dreadnought* in 1906 inspired the creation of their nickname.

Fifteen smaller double-deck cars entered traffic in 1901. They were built especially for service on the Marton route and were four-wheelers, unlike the bogie

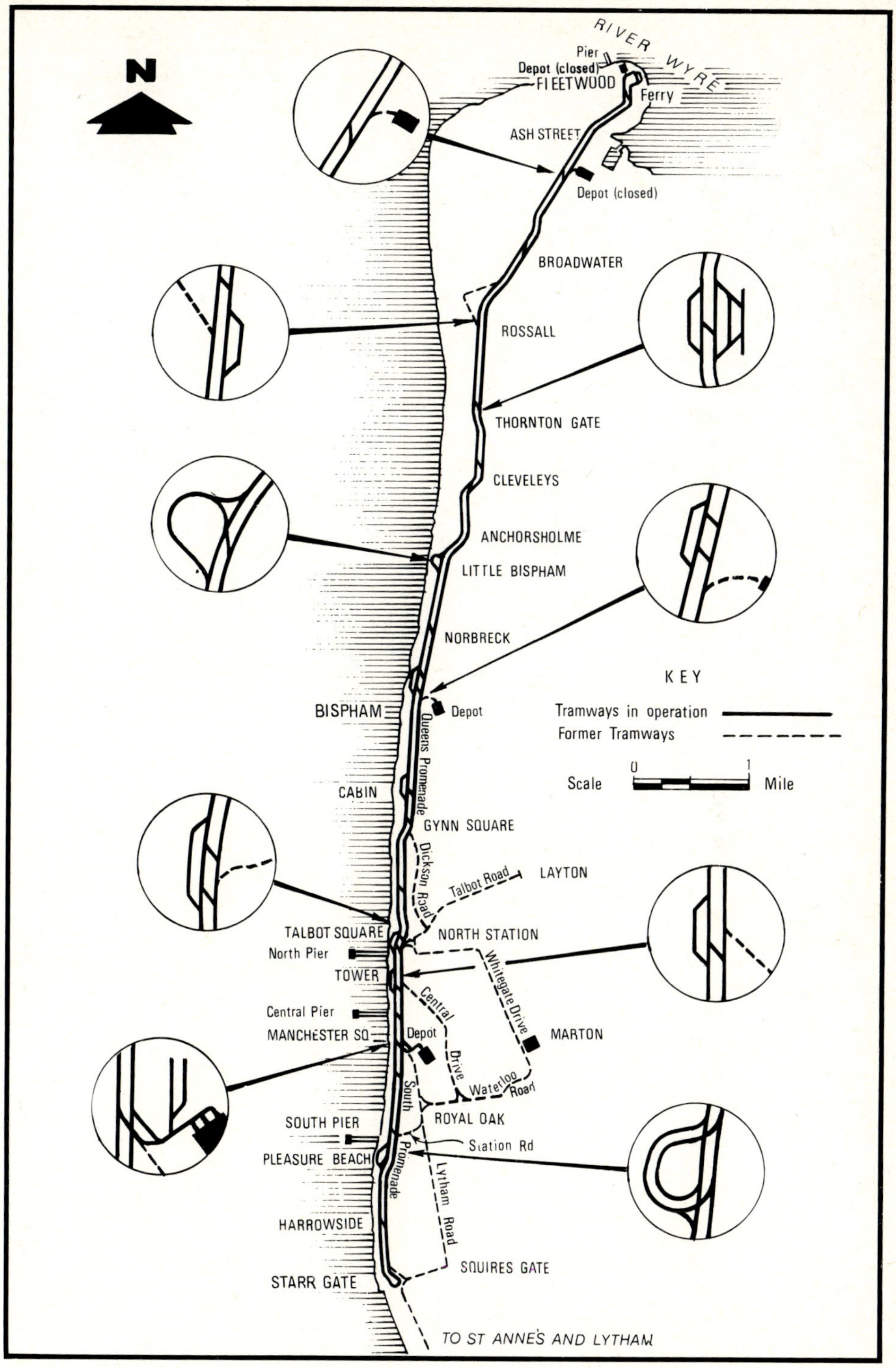

Above right:
Blackpool Corporation Tramway.

Right:
The tram which went to Crich, No 710, at the Pleasure Beach turning circle with No 762, the second 'Balloon' rebuild seen on 7 August 1983. In what is at the time of writing a non-standard livery, No 710 was sent to the National Tramway Museum in the summer of 1984 in part exchange for the preserved cars loaned for the Blackpool Centenary celebrations. It was built as an open-top car in 1934 and enclosed in 1941. *M. F. Haddon*

N

RIVER WYRE
Pier
Depot (closed)
FLEETWOOD
Ferry
ASH STREET
Depot (closed)
BROADWATER
ROSSALL
THORNTON GATE
CLEVELEYS
ANCHORSHOLME
LITTLE BISPHAM
NORBRECK
BISPHAM   Depot
CABIN
Queens Promenade
GYNN SQUARE
Dickson Road
Talbot Road   LAYTON
TALBOT SQUARE   NORTH STATION
North Pier
TOWER
Whitegate Drive
Central Pier
Central Drive
MANCHESTER SQ   Depot   MARTON
SOUTH PIER   Waterloo Road
ROYAL OAK
PLEASURE BEACH   Station Rd
South Promenade
HARROWSIDE   Lytham Road
STARR GATE   SQUIRES GATE
TO ST ANNE'S AND LYTHAM

KEY
Tramways in operation ———
Former Tramways – – –
Scale 0 ___ 1 Mile

5

Above:
No 717 was built as an enclosed car in 1934. It is shown at the Thornton Gate permanent way depot, three miles from Fleetwood. *Author*

Right:
A wet September day on the deserted Promenade as No 712 passes Manchester Square en route for Fleetwood. Built a year later than No 710, No 712 was also an open-top car until 1941. A number of cars have been fitted with pantograph current collectors. *Author*

Below right:
Brush 'Railcoach' No 626 in Fleetwood on one of the few remaining sections of genuine street tramway in the United Kingdom, 19 May 1972. *R. E. Ruffell*

'Dreadnoughts'. The opening of the Layton route in 1902 coincided with the delivery of 12 75-seat cars; they were not, however, intended specifically for this service, being designed to operate throughout the borough.

Widening of the Promenade commenced in 1902. As work progressed the tramway was moved onto its new reservation; by March 1904 the last single track section had been eliminated. Whilst this work was being undertaken the Blackpool, St Annes and Lytham Tramway Company made a connection to the Corporation's Lytham Road route at Squires Gate. The Lytham Company's (later the Lytham Corporation's) cars were to be seen in Blackpool until 1936.

Further additions to the fleet were made in 1911, when seven enclosed double-deck de-luxe cars entered traffic. They earned their de-luxe title by nature of the upholstery which covered the seats throughout. Three of them were four-wheelers, seating 66, whilst the rest were bogie vehicles seating 10 more. Between 1911 and 1914 the Corporation acquired 24 open bogie toastracks, cars which were to

leased by the Blackpool Electric Tramways Company; the remainder of the track was company-owned. In Blackpool it was mostly single with passing places, running through the streets between Talbot Road and Gynn Square; from here it was double-tracked throughout, running on a private reservation as far as Copse Road, Fleetwood where it became a street tramway again. At the time of the council takeover there was no physical connection with the Promenade tramway at Gynn Square.

When the tramroad opened there was none of the ribbon development along its route which is to be seen today; as an undertaking serving two centres, separated by largely rural terrain, it became one of the first British inter-urban tramroads. The line between Douglas and Ramsey on the Isle of Man, opened between 1893 and 1899, was a great influence on the Fleetwood promoters; some personnel were involved with both lines. (The Manx, in their turn, had been influenced by American practice).

By the end of the first operating season 19 cars had been delivered for use on the tramroad. The first 10 were open crossbench cars with seating for 48. Three

Above:
Street tramway in Blackpool: 'Railcoach' No 622 in Princes Parade. This car entered service in 1937 and from 1975 until it was damaged in an accident in 1980 carried an all-over livery advertising Blackpool Zoo. It received this modified livery when repairs were completed in 1983. A September 1983 view. *Author*

Right:
The 'Boats' are more often to be found in the depot than on the South Shore Promenade nowadays, but they do sometimes emerge on fine summer days and autumn evenings; they have been known to undertake tours of the illuminations! 17 August 1984. *M. F. Haddon*

Below right:
A tower-fitted road vehicle is put to good use as No 636's broken trolley pole is made safe before the car is towed ignominiously back to depot on 18 August 1984. *M. F. Haddon*

become as synonymous with the town as the 'Dreadnoughts'. Although they were only single deck vehicles, they were still capable of seating 69 passengers, the lack of a centre gangway providing the additional space required. The only second-hand members of the fleet were bought in 1919; they were six 69-seat double-deck cars built in 1901 for the London United Tramways in 1901. They survived at the seaside until 1934.

In 1920 the council bought the assets of the Blackpool & Fleetwood Tramroad Company. They included 41 cars, depots at Bispham, Copse Road and Fleetwood and slightly over eight miles of tramway. Opened in 1898, the tramroad started at Talbot Road station in Blackpool and served Bispham, Norbreck, Little Bispham, Anchorsholme, Cleveleys, Rossall and Broadwater before reaching Fleetwood. The track within the Blackpool borough boundary had been leased from the council, in the same way that the original Promenade tramway had been

Above:
For a few months of 1975 No 678 ran with an experimental pantograph installation. It is one of 10 'Railcoaches' converted for trailer towing and one of three which was never permanently coupled to its trailer. *Author*

Right:
A twinset with the trailer leading showing the destination Manchester Square, which probably meant it was returning to depot. As built the trailers had no controls; the need to turn the sets or run round the trailers to keep the motor cars leading was found to be less than convenient. From 1962 a programme of modifications was started, whereby the cars were permanently coupled and the control equipment from the inner end of the motor car was moved to the leading end of the trailer. The set seen here on 20 September 1984, motor car No 677 and trailer No 687, were the last to be dealt with, in 1970, leaving three sets untreated. *Author*

Below:
One-man car contrasts. These cars have also been rebuilt from 'Railcoaches', 13 being treated between 1972 and 1976. No 3 is seen on 21 September 1984 with a pantograph and No 6 with a roof advertising box, one of five of these cars so fitted. *Author*

The tramroad operated a basic 15min service throughout the year, with additional cars running as required, particularly during the summer, when frequency could be less than 4min. At really busy times cars could be turned round in 1½min, including unloading and loading and turning the trolley pole. This pattern of service was maintained throughout the tramroad's independent existence.

In was 1910 before any further cars were required. In that year three 64-seat opens were delivered; they were fitted with windscreens to protect the drivers. Following the example of the modified 1899

Above left:
No 641 is the latest addition to the fleet, the first completely new tram to be built for Blackpool since 1952, when the 'Coronations' went into traffic. It is shown in the Rigby Road depot on 20 September 1984. Behind it, by contrast, is the last of the 'Coronations' in service, although only on special occasions. Its 1952 livery was restored for the Centenary celebrations. *Author*

Left:
Rebuilt 'Balloons' Nos 761/2 seen at Bispham in September 1982. The positioning of the cars permits an examination of the more noticeable differences between them. Because of its centre exit No 762 can only accommodate 90 passengers instead of No 761's 98. Lighting, wipers and windows all owe their origins to commercial vehicle practice. *Author*

Below:
Unusually one-man car No 1 – seen on 21 September 1984 – wears a green and cream livery instead of the normal 'one-man' red and cream. The addition of a Blackpool produced pantograph makes this car the smartest and most distinctive of the one-man fleet. *Author*

open trailers followed, also seating 48; not having driving positions, they needed shunting at each terminus and proved to be difficult to operate. Withdrawn by 1902, they were soon to receive the necessary modifications which enabled them to operate as motor cars. The last six 1898 cars were enclosed vehicles, of similar capacity to the open stock. They were fitted with electric heating shortly after entering service.

Five more enclosed cars, with a different window layout to the first batch, but otherwise identical, were the first of 15 cars to be delivered in 1899. The second delivery that year was of another three open motor cars, similar to the first 1898 vehicles. The last seven 1899 cars were also opens, but of a different design and seating 55; roller shutters were added to these cars in 1907. (It should be noted that all the Fleetwood cars were single deckers and bogied).

From its opening the tramroad proved to be an immediate success, making an operating surplus of £8,584 in the first season; a year later a 10% dividend was paid to shareholders. Very quickly it was shown to be one of the most profitable transport undertakings in the country, with operational expenses being less than half of the gross income, a remarkable achievement. All additional investment made in the 20th century was made from reserves.

9

opens, they also were equipped with roller shutters. Their 64-seat capacity made them the largest in the fleet.

The last cars purchased by the tramroad company arrived in 1914. These were four enclosed vehicles which seated 48. They were of a similar appearance and layout to the enclosed cars delivered when the tramroad opened, although they came from a different builder. The main depot at Bispham, also the company's headquarters, was extended to accommodate them.

Reference has already been made to the line within the Blackpool Borough Council's boundary being held on a lease; it was due to expire in 1919. In 1918 the Bispham-with-Norbreck Urban District Council was amalgamated with Blackpool, extending the boundary nearly to Cleveleys. The council, wanting to control all public transport within its boundaries, intimated that it would not be renewing the tramroad company's lease; it was also proposing to undertake major developments along the cliffs which the tramroad ran on and wanted to keep any benefits for itself.

The mayor obtained options on a majority of the company's shares and offered them to the council at no profit to himself. Lacking the powers to operate the tramroad, the council then got the company to agree to operate the tramroad on its behalf until the necessary Act of Parliament had been obtained. The agreement, backdated to 1 January 1918, guaranteed the shareholders a 6½% tax free dividend, with the council taking any surplus; more than £3,000 in 1918. The legal requirements were completed the following year and the takeover became effective on 1 January 1920. The shareholders made a capital profit of £5 on each £10 share held.

As soon as the council took over, the tramroad was connected to the town's existing tramways. The line at Talbot Road station was extended to make a triangular

junction with the Layton route in Talbot Road and, more importantly, the tramway at Gynn Square was extended the short distance necessary to permit its connection to the tramroad. The cars were renumbered, although it was March before any of them were seen in corporation livery. The council closed the depots at Fleetwood terminus and Copse Road, Fleetwood, which had been used as running sheds, and concentrated tramroad operations at Bispham.

By the 1920s the Blackpool fleet had become a little tired. The newest vehicles had entered service in 1914 and the only ones withdrawn had been the old conduit cars. Some cars, dating from 1901/2 had been overhauled and modified to keep them in traffic after the end of World War 1, but even they weren't wearing too well. It was obvious that something drastic had to be done if services were to be maintained, yet the council would not authorise the purchase of new cars. The Tramway Department resorted to that old ploy, often

used by transport undertakings, the extensive rebuild.

To aid the operation an extensive workshop facility was installed on a new site in Rigby Road, adjoining the 1885 depot in Blundell Street. Work started in 1923. The cars involved dated from the turn of the century and even when rebuilt, with virtually all new components, they still retained some of their original design features. In some cases the only item reused was the roof, which was often the newest part of the original car. By the time the 'rebuild' programme had been completed in 1929, 42 'new' cars had been handed over to the traffic department; with 78 seats, they became the largest cars in the fleet. In addition, six genuine new cars, 64-seat open toastracks, had been built at the works in 1927. Of the 'new' cars, all except seven, built to the same slightly achaic design by a contractor, had been built by the council's own workforce. Numbering more than 100 at times, the men had achieved remarkable results, not only building new bodies, but

10

complete new chassis and bogies, except the wheels, as well. The only old cars still in traffic after their efforts were the 'Dreadnoughts'. By its own standards, even if not those of others, the Blackpool fleet had been thoroughly modernised.

The home-made 'Standard' trams were not the only new cars to be seen in Blackpool during the 1920s, for in 1928 delivery of 10 new single-deck 48-seat vehicles commenced. They were built for

Left:
Another depot scene shows twinset Nos 686/676, 'Boats' Nos 603/6/4/600, a trolley, rail grinder No 752 and overhead car No 753. In 1958 No 676 was the prototype twinset motor car. 'Boat' No 603, tucked away in the corner without its trolley tower, participated in the US Bicentennial celebrations in Philadelphia in 1976 and was still in the white and orange livery carried then; in February 1985 it was sold and exported to San Francisco. The other three 'Boats' are not in service, lacking trolley poles. The rail grinder, used for smoothing out track irregularities, was built in the undertaking's workshops in the 1920s or 1930s. No 753, a converted 'Standard' car of 1924, is used by the overhead maintenance team. The louvres in the window panels conceal the location of a diesel generator which can be used for propulsion, the car being fitted for overhead pickup as well. *Author*

Below left:
The location of the trams in the previous picture can be plotted on the disposition board; both were photographed on 21 September 1984. The Blundell Street depot is now demolished. *Author*

Above right:
No 634, advertising Blackpool Zoo since 1983, was given a Borough centenary livery in 1976 and from 1977 until 1981 advertised the Queen's Silver Jubilee; truly it is a versatile car. It is negotiating the Pleasure Beach turning circle on 18 August 1984. *M. F. Haddon*

Right:
No 633 has carried Post Office livery since 1982; it justifies its title when postal staff travel on it selling stamps. Special postmarks have been used on letters posted on the car; 17 August 1984. *M. F. Haddon*

Below:
No 632 has also been a liveried car since 1982, advertising a local brewery. Central Pier, 17 August 1984. *M. F. Haddon*

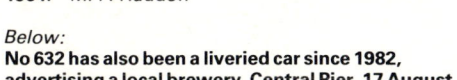

use on the Fleetwood tramroad and with their upholstered seats and rounded ends were considered to be the finest in the fleet.

The 1920s was also a period which saw a number of developments take place on both routes and services. In 1926 the Promenade tramway was extended southwards to Starr Gate; at that point a connection was made with the Lytham Corporation system. Other changes had no impact on route mileage but were to have a considerable effect on services. The tramroad route from Talbot Road station to Gynn Square was doubled and the connection of the Promenade tramway to the tramroad at the latter was improved; a severe dogleg in the tramroad at Rossall was straightened and the loop line to Fleetwood Ferry was installed. In consequence Promenade services were extended to Bispham, Lytham services to Gynn Square and some Fleetwood services were diverted to the Promenade where they terminated at the new South Beach turning circle.

The 1926 extension to the Promenade

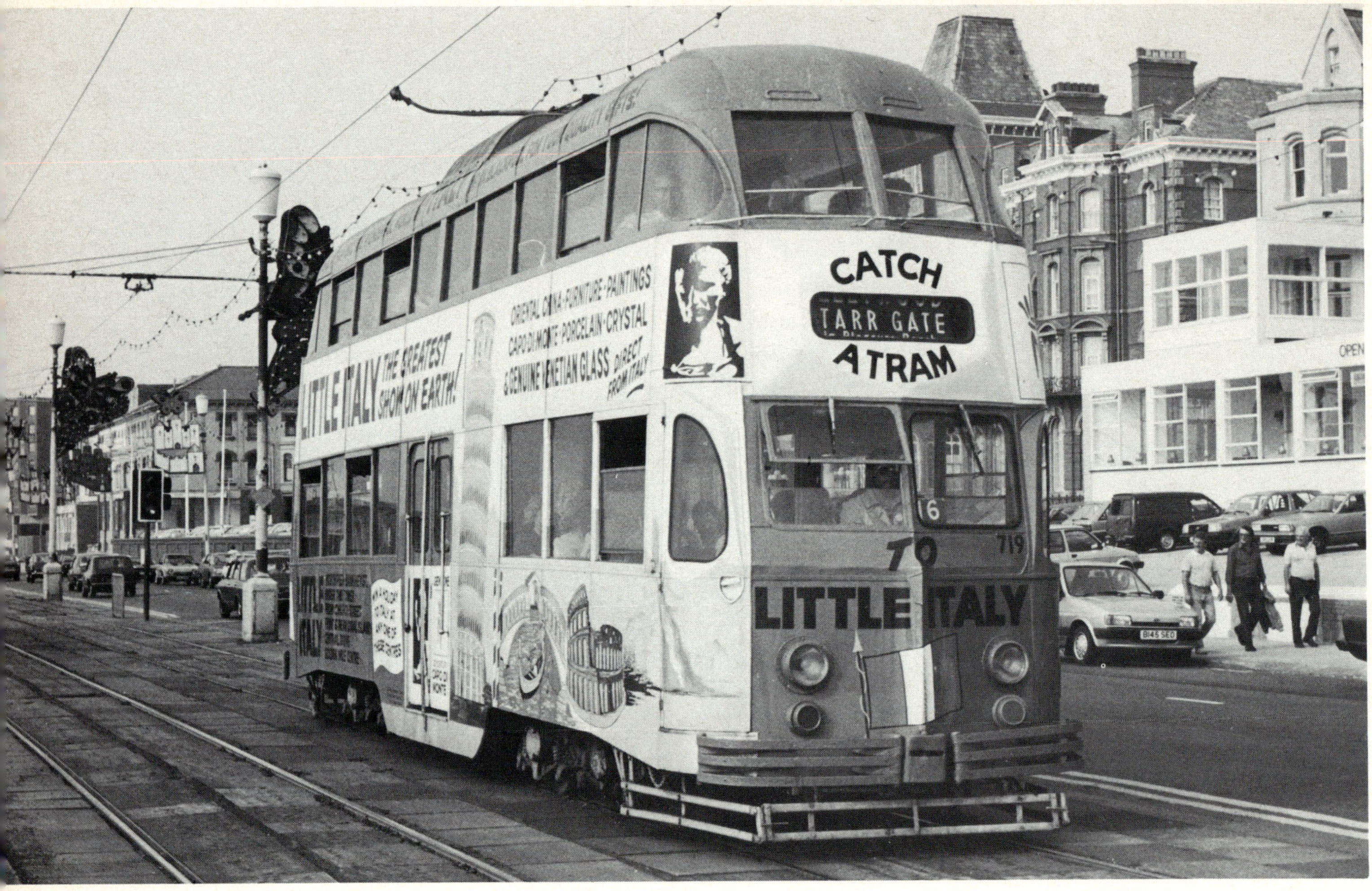

Above:
There are usually two 'Balloons' to be seen with an all-over advertisement. No 719 is shown here on 17 August 1984 with the third it has carried since 1981. *M. F. Haddon*

Right:
Tours of the illuminations start from the North Pier for the special cars. Here the Western Train, Nos 733/4, and the Rocket, No 732, await their customers at dusk on 20 September 1984. *Author*

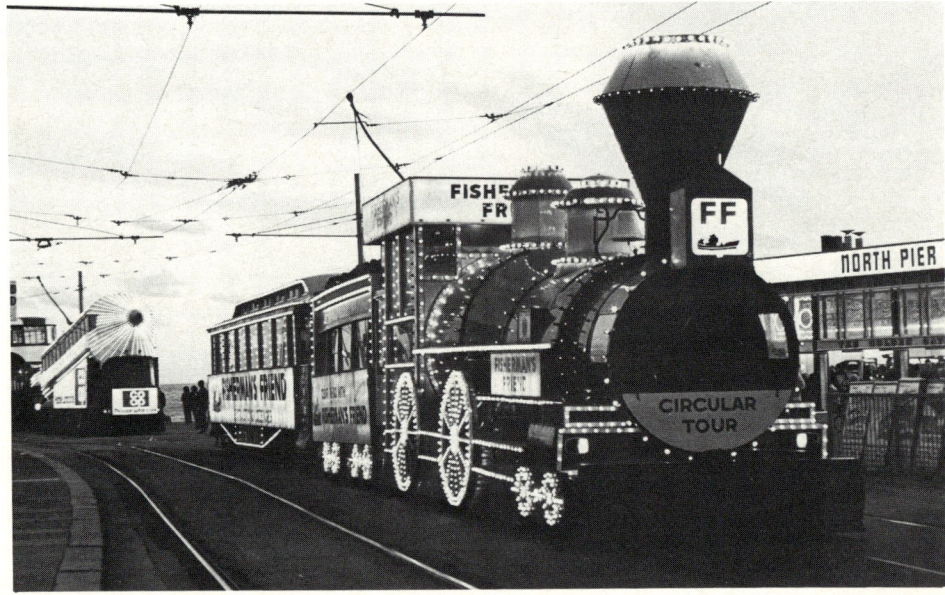

route was the last in Blackpool; it was followed 10 years later by the first closures. The Layton line and the Central Drive section of the Marton line were both victims of declining traffic on the town routes. However, in the 1930s the council made sufficient investment in the tramways to secure the future of at least part of the network until the present; by 1939 116 new modern trams had entered service. This new fleet was the result of a five-year plan which not only included modernising the fleet, but foresaw the eventual abandonment of all except the Promenade and Fleetwood routes.

The new cars were of several different types, although having the same basic modern streamlined appearance; all except 20 were built by English Electric. First to enter traffic were 25 'Railcoaches', single-deckers replacing Fleetwood cars. They introduced several new features, including heaters, clocks and opening 'sunshine' roofs. The 'Luxury Dreadnoughts' were 84-seat open-top double-deckers which eventually replaced the original 'Dreadnoughts'; the upper decks were enclosed, matching the otherwise similar 'Balloon' cars (14 of which were delivered in 1935) in 1942/3. All the double-deck cars had twin staircases. Electric footwarmers were a feature of the 'Luxury Toastracks' which also had enclosed sides, unlike the opensided toastracks they eventually superseded; these cars are now known as 'Boats', they seat 56. A further 20 'Railcoaches' were delivered by English Electric in 1935 but the firm must have been temporarily out of favour two years later, when Brush delivered a batch of 20 similar cars, built in such a way to avoid infringing English Electric's patents; they had electrically operated doors, initially driver, but later conductor controlled. The last cars to be delivered before the outbreak of war were known as 'Sun Saloons', although they could best be described as 'economy Railcoaches', being very basic in their fitting out. Apart from the Brush cars, all these additions to the Blackpool fleet had hand operated centre folding doors. With the delivery of the first 'Railcoaches' the fleet livery was changed from red and white to green and cream; this was simplified to green in 1941. Over 60 of these cars are still in traffic, some of them in much modified forms, but without them it is most unlikely that there would still be trams in Blackpool.

Tramcar developments after the war started with the last cars delivered before the war, the 'Sun Saloons'. In 1948 they were chosen to replace the home-made 'Standard' cars on the Marton route; to fit them for this duty they were overhauled and given upholstered seats and new control equipment. The conversion programme took until 1952, when the first totally new postwar trams were delivered. Naturally enough, these cars became known as 'Coronations'; they did not have a glorious reign. 25 of these 56 seat vehicles were built; they were fast, comfortable, heavy, subject to mechanical failure and expensive to operate. From 1964 some of these cars had

Left:
Two 'Standards', Nos 158/9, were fitted with lights in 1959. One of them is seen on normal duties on 16 July 1960. After withdrawal in 1966 one car was sold to the Tramway Museum Society for spares and the other went to the East Anglia Transport Museum. *R. Marshall*

Below:
'Dreadnought' No 59 on 16 July 1960 as it was restored for the 75th anniversary in 1960. Since then it has been restored a second time, participating in the Borough centenary celebrations in 1976 and being used for tours and charters since. It was one of the big attractions of the tramway centenary. *R. Marshall*

their control equipment replaced with that from withdrawn vehicles; this did not ensure their survival, however, for the first withdrawals took place in 1968; the last in traffic were withdrawn in 1975, by which time most had been scrapped.

An experiment with trailer operation took place in 1958, when two 'Railcoaches' were rebuilt with 'Coronation' type ends and coupled together. Their entry to traffic, mainly on tours, did not generate any objections, unlike their 1885 predecessors, so it was decided to convert a total of 10 'Railcoaches' as towing vehicles and to order 10 66-seat trailers. They entered traffic in 1960, in time for the town to

celebrate the 75th anniversary of its tramways.

The transport committee decided to have a procession of trams; scattered about the system were a number of remarkable relics of the past and it was decided that they should be restored for the cavalcade. There was No 4, an original conduit car which had survived as a tower wagon; Blackpool & Fleetwood No 2 of 1898, an open toastrack which had survived as a snow plough; Blackpool & Fleetwood No 40 of 1914, which had spent many years as a personnel carrier for the Permanent Way Department; and 'Dreadnought' No 59 of 1902, saved from being scrapped in 1935.

On 29 September 1960 these veterans led a procession of 11 cars from the Pleasure Beach to Little Bispham. As part of the celebrations all except No 4 ran in traffic for varying periods. Afterwards they were all put into store for two or three years before being donated to the embryo National Tramway Museum at Crich.

The restored cars were not the only non-standard trams to be seen in Blackpool in 1960, for there were also three feature vehicles in service. The oldest, the Venetian gondola, had been brought out for the annual illuminations since 1925. The lifeboat was a year younger; both were built as non-passenger carrying illuminated cars constructed on the chassis of withdrawn vehicles, later suitable openings were cut in their sides so that passengers could board without need of a ladder. The *Blackpool Belle*, a Mississippi paddle steamer, carried passengers from the beginning and was built in 1959. Service cars had sometimes been trimmed with lights, either just for the effect or for special events; the last of these

Blackpool Centenary

Below right:
Blackpool's tramway centenary was celebrated, on 29 September 1985, with a cavalcade of trams, both ancient and modern. Prior to the anniversary Blackpool Transport organised a full programme of events, starting with a guided tour of the undertaking's works on 18 May; the tours were repeated each month until the final celebrations in September. Additionally further events were held, centreing on the visiting trams and the depot. The first of these took place on 16 June when the depot was opened to the public and Blackpool No 40, Edinburgh No 35 and Glasgow No 1297 ran trips between Talbot Square and the depot. For enthusiasts the chance of riding on a vintage tram over non-Promenade tracks was too good to be missed; the 20p single fare was cheaper than the stage fare for the journey, too! On 14 July Lord Street, Fleetwood, was closed to traffic and services were operated by the vintage fleet, supported by vintage commercial vehicles. Further tramway events were held in conjunction with the Blackpool Karneval Week in August.

Before the visitors arrived at the depot open day on 16 June, the oldest car, Blackpool Electric Tramway Company No 4, was shunted into position by No 706, newly converted to open top condition. *Author*

Above left:
Open-top No 706 passes No 167, built for the Fleetwood service in 1927 and preserved at the National Tramway Museum, cross in Lord Street, Fleetwood on Sunday 14 July 1985. The Blackpool & Fleetwood Transport Festival caused the road to be closed to the exclusion of all traffic except the historic trams and preserved commercial vehicles.
Author

Above:
In front of the depot it was possible to compare a 'Luxury Dreadnought' with the surviving original 'Dreadnought'. Also on the depot frontage on 16 June were Bolton No 66 and Manchester No 765. Sheffield No 513 and Blackpool No 167 were displayed alongside the fitting shop, in Blundell Street. *Author*

Right:
At Talbot Square Blackpool No 40 waited to return to the depot as Edinburgh No 35 arrived. A siding was laid in her so that preserved trams could be put on display out of the way of the service cars. *Author*

were 'Standards' Nos 158/9 which were illuminated in 1959 and remained in service until 1966. From 1961 new passenger carrying feature cars were introduced; in 1961 a rocket, in 1962 a Western train (complete with both locomotive and carriage), in 1963 the Hovertram and in 1965 HMS *Blackpool*. The gondola and lifeboat were withdrawn in 1962 and 1961 and the *Blackpool Belle* in 1978.

Route closures commenced in 1961 with the withdrawal of services along Lytham Road, to Squires Gate, and Station Road, between South station and the Promenade. The Marton route followed in 1962 and the Tramroad line between North station and Gynn Square in 1963, leaving only the 11½-mile coastal route from Starr Gate to Fleetwood.

Tram withdrawals were also taking place during the 1960s, until by 1967 only cars from the 1930s five-year plan survived to operate the remaining route. This did not mean that tramcar development ceased, for new ways of improving the efficiency of the undertaking were continuously sought. In 1969 a Brush 'Railcoach' was modified for one-man operation. In itself it was not a success but it did lead the way for further developments. The availability of the Bus Grant for new vehicles suitable for one man operation proved to be a spur, especially when confirmation was received that it would apply to new trams! Between 1972 and 1976 13 'railcoaches' were modified by lengthening to make room for a front entrance. Because the bogie centres were unchanged the ends were tapered to avoid conflicts on curves. To distinguish them from the crew-operated cars they were turned out in a yellow and crimson livery; they are now painted red and cream. The one-man cars are used throughout the year, their main purpose being the winter service to Fleetwood.

By the end of the 1970s the majority of the fleet was nearly 40 years old and it was necessary to consider ways of modernising or replacing it; a conundrum given that the constraints on finance meant that any solution had to be both cost effective whilst taking advantage of modern technology. Two prototypes were built, the first being ready for service in 1979. Numbered 761, its modern appearance belied its origins as a 'Balloon' conversion. It owed its appearance to the use of standard commercial vehicle parts which could be readily obtained and, in some cases, were common to spares already kept for the council's buses. The fitting of bus type windows made it difficult to distinguish road from rail at a distance! The intention of operating 'driver only' made a combined entry/exit, with power doors, a feature. Seating was provided for 98. Thanks to an offer from Westinghouse new control equipment was installed; in addition to being economical in power consumption it gave the vehicle smooth acceleration and braking. No 761 had been in service for over a year when construction of the second prototype, No 762, commenced. As a result a number of modifications were made, the most obvious being the provision of a centre exit, for No 761 had proved to be too slow in loading and unloading; in consequence capacity was reduced to 90. Other changes included the installation of Brush electrical control equipment and the use of rebuilt bogies. Like No 761 and the one-man conversions, No 762 was built in the Rigby Road works. It was handed over to the Traffic Department in 1982.

The experience gained with Nos 761 and 762 proved to be most valuable but they, or vehicles like them, were not seen to be the ideal solution for year-round Fleetwood services. The extensive use to which the one-man trams are put is responsible for both increased wear and maintenance costs. Replacements were needed but the cost of new cars from a continental builder, about £300,000 each, was too high, and Rigby Road works didn't have the capacity to build entirely new cars within the time-scale required. It was decided that 10 cars were needed, that the bodies should be built by a bus builder, the bogies by a local engineering company and that assembly, including installation of the electrical equipment, should be carried out at Rigby Road. The order for a prototype was placed in 1982 and it is expected that, following evaluation, further orders will be placed for three annual batches of three cars although the situation is unclear as this is written, it being reported that further construction has been cancelled. No 641 went into service in June 1984; costing about £140,000, it has seating for 55 passengers and, like Nos 761 and 762, has fixed seating, mostly facing forwards at the back and rearwards at the front. Unlike No 762, the centre exits are offset, making unloading easier for the driver to observe.

An interesting development was announced in 1985; it entails the council leasing a new tram from GEC Traction. The car, No 651, has the same body style as No 641 but its GEC electrical equipment is experimental, enabling the company to test it under realistic conditions. It was delivered in April 1985.

In 1981 a Blackpool councillor was looking forward to the tramway's centenary in 1985, and suggested that restored trams from museums should run in the town as part of the celebrations. Those involved in restoring Bolton No 66, a double-deck bogie car of 1902 vintage, then nearly complete after 18 years' effort, suggested that their car could be borrowed as a trial. The offer was accepted and the car moved to Blackpool in June that year. It has since earned its keep on charters and illuminations tours, as well as the occasional service duty. Other participants were Edinburgh No 35 (in Blackpool from 1983), Glasgow No 1297 (in Blackpool from 1984), Hill of Howth (Eire) No 10, Manchester No 765 and Sheffield No 513 (in Blackpool from 1984). Some preserved Blackpool cars also appeared; No 4 (running on batteries to maintain its appearance as a conduit car), No 40 (a 'Standard' in red livery) and No 167 (a Fleetwood saloon). 'Dreadnought' No 59 which returned for the Borough centenary in 1976 also appeared. The undertaking itself provided the last service 'Coronation', restored to 1953 condition, and 'Balloons' Nos 706 and 712, restored to open top condition (modern safety standards preclude a restoration to exact 1934 appearance) and to 1935 condition internally, respectively. To make room for the visiting trams some service cars had to be outstationed at lending museums; 'Balloon' No 710 transferred to Crich in 1984 and 'Boats' Nos 600 and 607 went to Heaton Park and Crich during 1985. There can be no doubt that the centenary was even more memorable than the 75th Anniversary and that the Blackpool undertaking is one with a future.

Left:
Another Blackpool contribution to the centenary celebrations is the restoration of No 706 to open-top condition. The car had been out of service following an accident in 1980. Work had not been completed when the photograph was taken on 21 September 1984. Alongside is Glasgow No 1297, loaned from Crich and arriving in Blackpool in April 1984, since when it has been used in a similar manner to the other preserved cars. It is a 70-seat vehicle built in 1948. *Author*

BRITISH TRAMS & TRAMWAYS in the 1980s

Isle of Man

The transport systems in the Isle of Man are remarkable in both their variety and the longevity of their rolling stock. Those to be considered here, the tramways, whilst being obviously different, have unbelievably complex and intertwined histories; the accounts which follow are therefore necessarily condensed. The lines are reviewed in geographical order, starting at the island's capital, Douglas, and working northwards.

Douglas Corporation

The only Manx rail services not operated by the nationalised Isle of Man Railways Board are the horse trams operated by Douglas Corporation. The two-mile long 3ft gauge Promenade tramway was opened in sections in 1976/7 and 1890, following a route around Douglas Bay.

The tramway was privately promoted by Thomas Lightfoot, a retired contractor from Sheffield. At the time Douglas was in the throes of becoming a typical Victorian

seaside resort. The opening of Loch Promenade in 1875 provided the impetus to Lightfoot and gave him the idea of constructing a tramway along it.

Construction started from Burnt Mill Hill, to the north of the bay, and worked southwards. When the official opening took place in 1876, the line was complete as far as the Iron Pier. The remainder of the route southwards to Victoria Pier was opened in January 1877. The line was single with passing loops and was provided with three cars built in Birkenhead. Two were open-top double-deckers for summer use, whilst

Left:
The Isle of Man Tramways: Manx Electric Railway, Snaefell Mountain Railway and the Douglas Horse Tramway.

Below:
A distinctive feature of the Douglas system is the provision of low level traffic lights which only apply to the horse trams, shown here at the junction of Central Promenade and Broadway in May 1983. *Author*

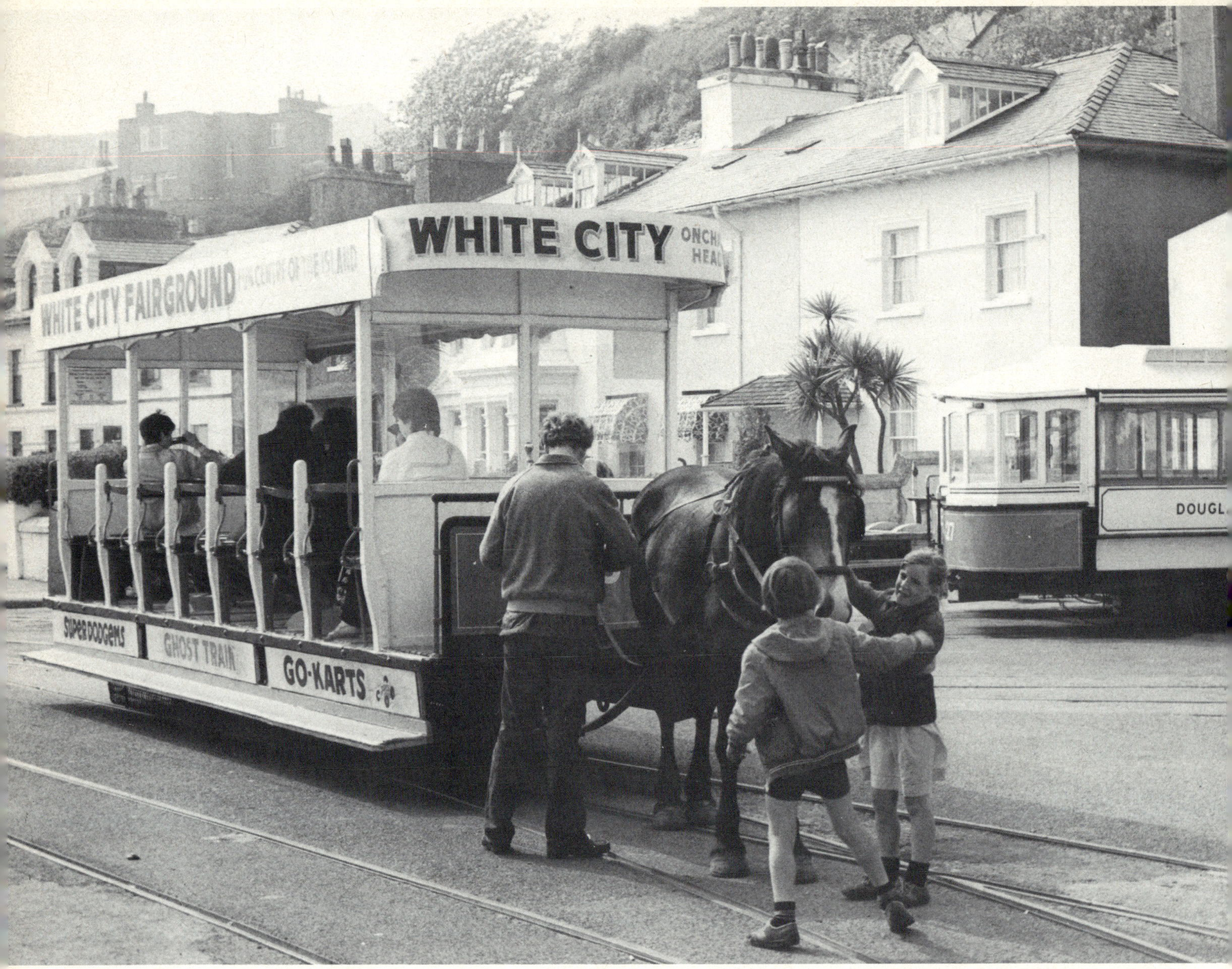
WHITE CITY
WHITE CITY FAIRGROUND
SUPER DODGEMS
GHOST TRAIN
GO-KARTS

SHOP & TRAM DISPLAY
TERMINUS TAVERN
Stones
TERMINUS BUILDING
TRAM Souvenir SHOP

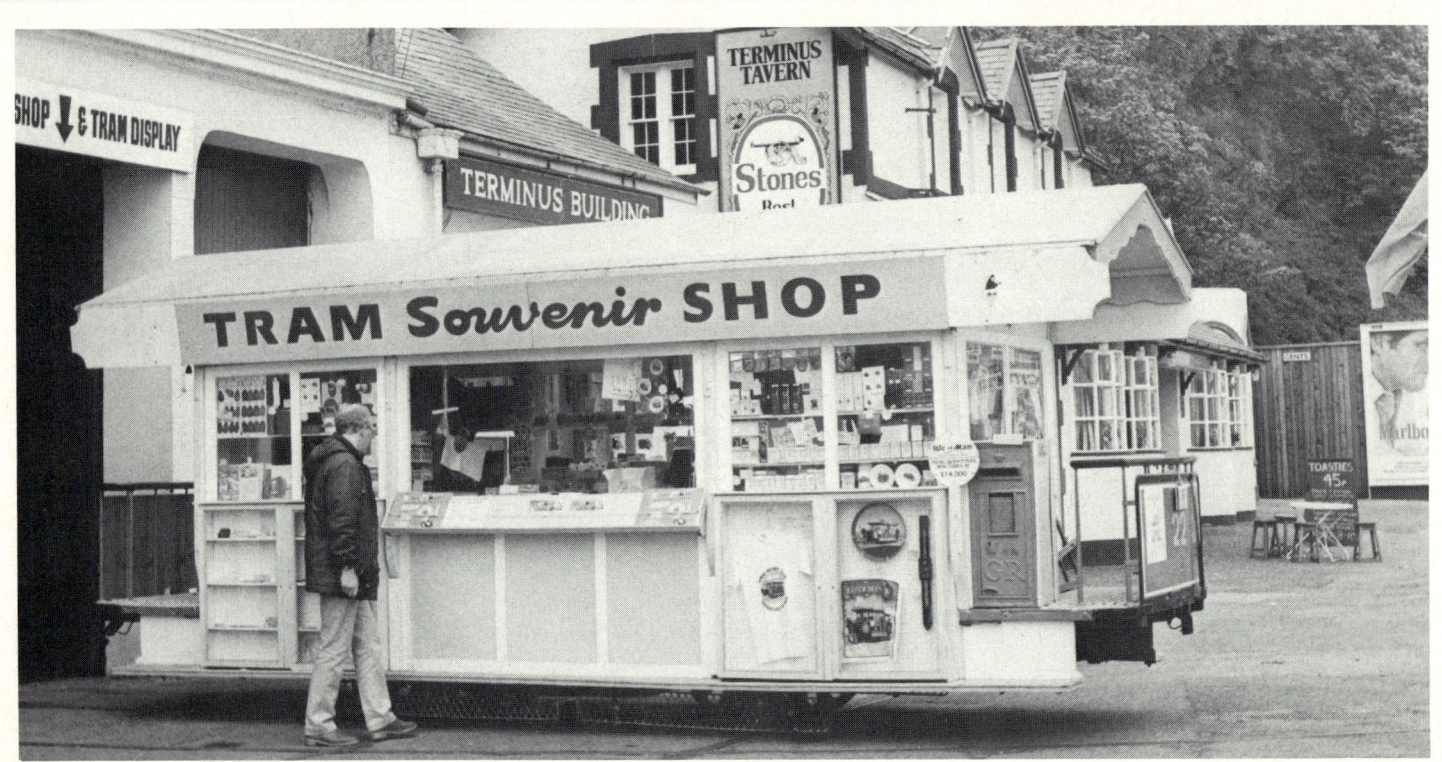

the third was an enclosed saloon designed for winter use. A further double-deck car was obtained in 1882. In that year Lightfoot's financial resources were stretched by a theatre development he was involved in, so he sold the tramway to the newly formed Isle of Man Tramways Ltd.

The company proceeded to increase the capacity of the line by installing more passing loops and purchasing more cars. The northern extension to Derby Castle was opened in 1890; a large depot was built there, to replace the original one at the former Burnt Mill Hill. Where the width of the Promenade allowed, and where permission could be obtained, sections of track were doubled to further increase capacity.

In 1894 the tramway was sold again, this time to the Douglas & Laxey Coast Electric Tramway Co Ltd. This company was just in the process of opening the electric line to Laxey; in view of its widened responsibilities and objectives it was restructured and became the Isle of Man Tramways and Electric Power Co Ltd. The new management improved the Derby Castle depot and built a joint station for both the horse and electric cars. Further track doubling was carried out in 1897 when plans to electrify the Promenade route were revealed. Council approval was obtained, only to be withdrawn following objections from residents (objecting to the wires) and cab men (objecting to the competition).

The tramway changed hands for the last time in 1902. The earlier collapse of Dumbell's Bank caused the Isle of Man Tramways & Electric Power Co to be liquidated. The new owner was Douglas Corporation.

Proposals to electrify the line were given further consideration by the corporation, prompted in the main by the Manx Electric Railway Co; they were finally rejected in 1908. Despite this refusal to modernise the line, the corporation did continue to invest in it. New cars were bought, older ones were fitted with roller bearings, the track was relaid and eventually doubled throughout. Profits were made each year, even during the depression, although the winter service was withdrawn in 1927.

By the time the tramway celebrated its 75th anniversary in 1949 the last of the double-deck cars had been withdrawn, one being kept for preservation, initially in England. There were 33 cars in service, the newest being built in 1935.

When the centenary arrived it was celebrated in fine style, including the issue of a set of stamps by the Manx postal authority. The last double-deck car returned to the island and participated in a tramcar parade, as did the restored Douglas cable car, propelled by a Land Rover. These two cars became the foundation of a small museum collection at the Derby Castle Depot and are now to be seen with No 12, the oldest surviving vehicle in near original condition; it was built in 1888. Three other cars, Nos 11, 47 and 49 are to be seen in the electric railway museum at Ramsey. At Derby Castle No 22 has become a tram shop, selling souvenirs to visitors. No 31 is no longer a passenger car, although it is sometimes to be seen on the Promenade, for it now carries advertising hoardings.

In 1981 the Douglas horse trams made a loss for the first time in their history but services still continue as before. The fleet is now reduced to 21 service cars which look set to see many years of operations in the future.

Finally, a word about the motive power. The horses on the day shift work no more than four trips a day, whilst the more experienced animals used on the evening shift may work up to six trips. In the off-peak season they work two days in three and in the peak they work six days a week. Lightfoot's original stables on Queens Promenade are still in regular use; resting animals are put out to grass, as they all are during the winter. Until 1974 new stock was bought annually from Ireland. In that year the price nearly doubled so the Corporation decided to establish a stud from the existing animals, of which there are now about 60. Each horse has a working life of approximately seven years.

Manx Electric Railway

The first section of the Manx Electric Railway was opened in 1893. Two miles long, it ran from Derby Castle, at the northern end of Douglas Bay, to Groudle. It was single track with two passing places when opened, the second track being brought into use the following year. Those developing the Howstrake estate, through which the line ran, considered that their efforts would meet with greater success if public access were facilitated. The tramway was authorised in a clause which also covered the provision of water, gas, electricity and drains!

By the time of the opening the promoters had extended their vision somewhat, floating a company called the Douglas & Laxey Coast Electric Tramway Co Ltd. An abbreviated version, Douglas & Laxey Coast Electric Tramway, was emblazoned on the side of the three motor cars and six trailers obtained for the opening of the Groudle line.

The extension to Laxey, 4½ miles from Groudle, was opened in the summer of 1894. The Douglas horse trams were taken over at the same time so the company was restructured, becoming the Isle of Man Tramways & Electric Power Co Ltd. To operate the additional mileage to Laxey a further six motor cars and six trailers were delivered. Although built in England, all the tramway's cars clearly had their origins in current American practice for interurban lines. Both batches of trailers had open

sides, the second delivery being more adaptable to varying weather conditions by having side curtains.

Following the promotion of several different routes by different groups, official sanction was obtained for an extension to Ramsey, 10.75 miles, in 1897. Three steam engines were used by the construction teams, including one each hired from the Isle of Man Railway and the Manx Northern Railway. The new line was opened to within a mile of the proposed Ramsey terminus in 1898, the last section being opened a year later. More rolling stock was delivered, so that by the turn of the century the company owned 20 motor cars and 18 trailers. A particularly interesting item of rolling stock was a home-made electric locomotive. It consisted of a centre-cab superstructure only, being given the bogies and electrical controller from a passenger car when it was required for use. It was used for both track work and handling freight traffic. It was damaged in a collision in 1914 and lay out of use until it was rebuilt, incorporating two wagon bodies, in 1926.

As already mentioned in the account of

Above left:
Car No 2, built in 1893, posed on 28 May 1983 on the Ramsey side of Laxey with an open trailer. The livery is that of the Douglas & Laxey Coast Electric Tramway. A Snaefell car is to be seen immediately above, with the Snaefell car shed to the left. *Author*

Left:
Car No 1 is now also in similar condition and livery to No 2; here it is seen at Derby Castle depot as it was on 9 August 1975. *M. F. Haddon*

Above:
Car No 5 was built in 1894 as a 32-seat vehicle. It is shown at Laxey on 28 May 1983 in The Manx Electric Railway Co Ltd livery. *Author*

Right:
No 9, also built in 1894 but with 36 seats, is shown on 13 August 1975 in the livery carried by all the stock until the historical liveries programme was instituted. The combination is crossing Maughold Road, close to its Ramsey destination. The gradient behind the trailer is noticeably steep. *M. F. Haddon*

the Douglas horse trams, the collapse of Dumbell's Bank in 1900 forced the company into liquidation. It was revealed that it was under capitalised, the shortfall being met by the bank, which had borrowed to fulfill the company's requirement. It took two years to sort out its affairs so it was not until 1902 that the liquidator was able to find a customer for the electric tramways, including the Snaefell line; they were sold to the Manx Electric Railway Co.

The new company found that there was much to do to bring the line up to scratch. It replaced the electricity generating and transmission system; it overhauled the track and bought six motor cars and 10 trailers. A new depot was built at Laxey. In 1904 the purchase of the Manx Northern Railway was considered but nothing came of it, the railway going to the Isle of Man Railway instead. In the following years the company invested in local tourist attractions, glens and tea houses, and ran combined tours involving them and the tramway. So that it controlled all aspects of the tours the company bought its own charabancs.

Until World War 1 losses were made on operating, a situation aggravated by dividend payments on preference shares and debentures. After the war operating was more successful; attempts were made to reduce the debenture burden but little progress was made. By 1935 the payment of debenture interest was two years in arrears, albeit on a reduced issue.

A fire at Laxey in 1930 destroyed 11 cars; it must be indicative of a decline in traffic that eight of them were not replaced. The three trailers bought at this time were the last supplied to the tramway.

Rising costs forced the company to cease generating its own electricity in 1934, a

supply being taken, subsequently, from the Isle of Man Electricity Board. The company had previously supplied electricity to customers in the Onchan and Derby Castle areas.

The number of passengers carried was reduced by the second war; as a bonus some freight traffic was generated by it. It proved possible to make economies in operating so that by 1945 the tramway was much healthier financially. The increase in traffic that year produced an operating surplus of £11,000. The inclusive tours were resumed in 1946; increased competition on the roads reduced demand, however, and they weren't offered after 1952. The company-owned buses were sold in 1953.

Riding on the wave of its postwar success, the company was restructured in 1949. The following year there was a big slump in passengers and the small profit made was insufficient to meet debenture interest. In 1953 an operating loss was made. The debenture holders benefitted from the sale of property assets.

In 1955 the island government was asked if it would buy the tramway assets for £70,000. At that point it was proposed to close the lines the following autumn. Counter-proposals and negotiations were protracted. Powers to abandon were applied for in July 1956; Tynwald refused to grant them. It did make an offer, by which

the company agreed to operate during 1957 with the support of government indemnification against losses. Later that year an offer of £50,000, estimated to be the scrap value of the infrastructure, was made. Accepted by the company and later enacted by Tynwald, it was arranged that the undertaking would change hands on 1 June 1957.

From that date both the tramway and the Snaefell line were controlled by the Manx Electric Railway Board of Tynwald. A schedule of renewals was drawn up and the first two miles of track were relaid during the winter of 1957/8. The worst sections were the oldest, between Douglas and Laxey. A new livery of green and cream was implemented but did not wear well and was abandoned within two years. Following a report on the financial situation, in 1958, the wisdom of retaining the Laxey-Ramsey section was debated. It was saved by a close vote but the matter was to be debated further in both the 1960s and the 1970s.

Under the new management passenger traffic fluctuated, although tending to increase. A new station building was opened at Ramsey in 1964. The Derby Castle-Laxey relaying was completed in 1965 and some resleepering was done on the Laxey-Ramsey section. The goods collection and delivery service was withdrawn in 1966; parcels were still carried subject to the recipient being willing to collect. In 1972 another non-passenger service was withdrawn; this was the clearance of lineside postboxes by the conductors. Introduced in 1903, the service was withdrawn because of a proposal to reduce winter operations; in consequence the boxes could not be emptied at the times agreed with the Post Office.

The reduced winter services were themselves withdrawn in 1975, coinciding with the closure of the Laxey-Ramsey section. The loss of traffic caused by the closure was more than anticipated; following extensive consideration of the matter, the line was reopened in 1977, following an extensive programme of refurbishment. The Isle of Man Railway was taken over by the Government the same year, the Manx Electric Railway Board taking responsibility for its operation. The nationalised Douglas Corporation bus services were also placed in the care of the Board, which in 1982 was restructured as the Isle of Man Transport Board.

The centenary of electric railways was a cause for celebration in 1979, when four service cars were restored to old liveries and ran in a cavalcade at Laxey. Two non-passenger vehicles, the electric locomotive and a bogie freight car, were restored for the cavalcade and placed in the museum at Ramsey which was opened afterwards.

The cavalcade became the forerunner of the type of event laid on as part of the annual Vintage Transport Weekend; held each spring, the weekends involve all aspects of Manx transport and give enthusiasts the opportunity to explore those nooks and crannies of the systems which are not usually available to the public. On the tramway participants have access to the depots at Derby Castle and Laxey and special tours are run using vintage liveried cars (more have been reliveried since 1979) which stop for photography at strategic places.

Although the Manx Electric Railway cars are outwardly much the same as they have always been, changes have taken place

Above:
Whilst No 23 was operating Car No 33 was confined to depot, for the locomotive was using No 33's bogies. Seen at Derby Castle depot, No 33 was built as a 56-seat vehicle in 1906. *Author*

Left:
Locomotive No 23 normally resides in the Ramsey museum, where it keeps company with three Douglas horse trams and bogie freight trailer No 26. The latter started life as a passenger car in 1895, was stored from 1902 and converted to freight use in 1918. It was last used in 1944. *Author*

Below:
An addition to the museum collection was made after the Ramsey Pier Railway was closed in 1981. The rolling stock was given to the Ramsey Commissioners for a proposed line in a park. When this failed to come to fruition it was given to the Isle of Man Railway Society, which maintains the museum. The locomotive, a Planet built by Hibberd in 1937, was made operational in 1985 so that the ensemble could make demonstration runs on a short section of the electric railway. *Author*

which bring them to the edge of modern technology. Roller bearing motors, air whistles, speedometers and radios have been fitted, the latter replacing the telephones formerly used to control operations, they have the advantage of improving system flexibility, too. The motors are actually extensive rebuilds of those supplied with the cars; given the way the Manx look after their electrical equipment, there is no reason why they should not last as long rebuilt as they did before.

The Manx Government has made a considerable investment in its electric railway over the years; there is obviously considerble political motivation to keep the system going. This being so we can surely look forward to the MER centenary, in 1993, with every confidence.

Snaefell Mountain Railway

The railway to the summit of Snaefell, 2,034ft above sea level, was opened in 1895. It was a private promotion by a group of individuals with various interests in the Isle of Man, including the electric railway, then newly opened to Laxey. The mountain line, 4½ miles long, was 3ft 6in gauge, 6in wider than the Manx standard of 3ft. The extra inches were to accommodate the Fell patent braking system; the cars carried brake wheels underneath which gripped a centre rail. Construction was remarkably quick, only seven months being taken. A locomotive, *Caledonia*, was hired from the Manx Northern Railway to haul works trains, a third rail being laid temporarily. A double track was laid, mostly with a gradient of 1 in 12. The influence of those involved with the coastal line was enough to ensure that electricity was used to power the mountain cars. Six of these were delivered for the opening, in appearance similar to their contemporaries, Nos 10-13 on the electric railway. The Laxey terminus was close to the car shed, a distance away from the other Laxey station; in 1897 the Snaefell line was extended slightly and a joint station was created.

The Summit station was graced with a hotel which only served to provide shelter and refreshments to visitors. The building, whose opening coincided with that of the railway, was a timber structure; a larger, more substantial building replaced it in 1906. This structure survived until it was gutted by fire in 1982. Temporary facilities, including a siding and a crossover, were provided whilst a new hotel was built. It opened in 1984, nearly two years after the fire.

A year after the opening the enterprise was sold to the Isle of Man Tramways & Electric Power Co, the owners of the coastal electric railway. The terms, nearly double the cost of construction and equipment, were most equitable for the promoters; even the company made a substantial profit on its £2,000 investment in the mountain.

Once established, the Snaefell line settled into its intended routine of carrying visitors to the summit and back. The only interruption was when road racing closed the line at the Bungalow. By the time it, with the Manx Electric Railway, was nationalised in 1957, it appeared little different from the turn of the century. The MER Board instituted a programme of track renewals and increased the publicity the line received, nearly doubling the number of passengers carried.

In 1970 Car No 5 was damaged in a fire at the summit. It was rebuilt without a clerestory and with bus type windows, the work being carried out at Ramsey; it re-entered service the following year. (All Manx electric cars are normally maintained at the MER depot at Derby Castle; Snaefell cars travel there on electric railway bogies, a mixed gauge siding being provided at Laxey for changeover purposes). Until 1977 the Snaefell cars were still using their original motors. As the cost of maintaining them was increasing, in line, it seemed, with a decrease in reliability, it was decided to install modern equipment. The cost of

Right:
The rebuilt No 5 near the Snaefell car shed and with the Laxey wheel in the background, 28 May 1983. *Author*

Below:
Laxey joint station on 28 May 1983 shows from the left: trailer No 41, built 1930, at the rear of a combination bound for Douglas; Car No 5 bound for Ramsey; and Snaefell cars Nos 1 and 2. The siding on which No 1 stands is dual gauge. No 2 is fitted with a headlamp from an Aachen car. *Author*

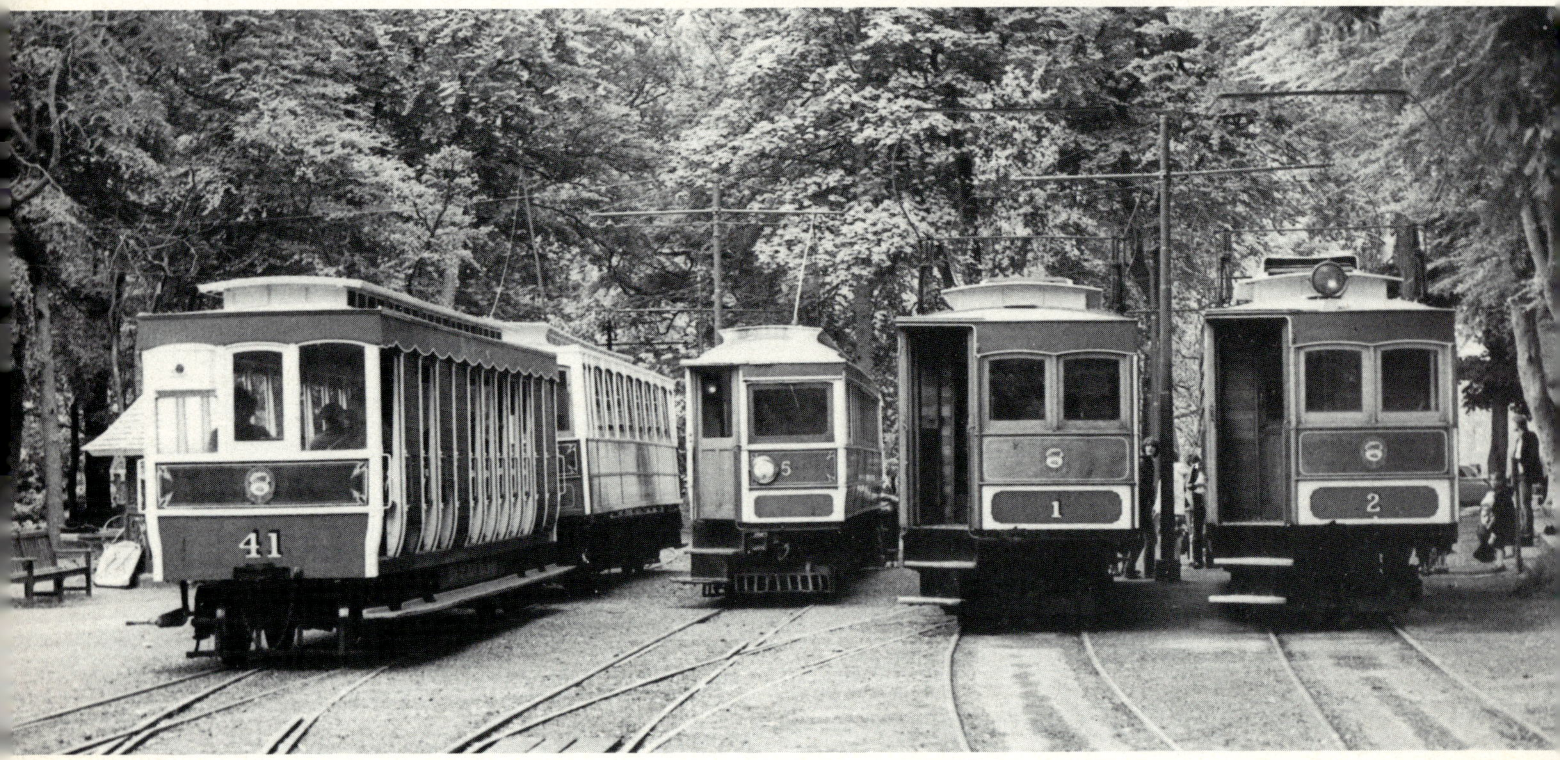

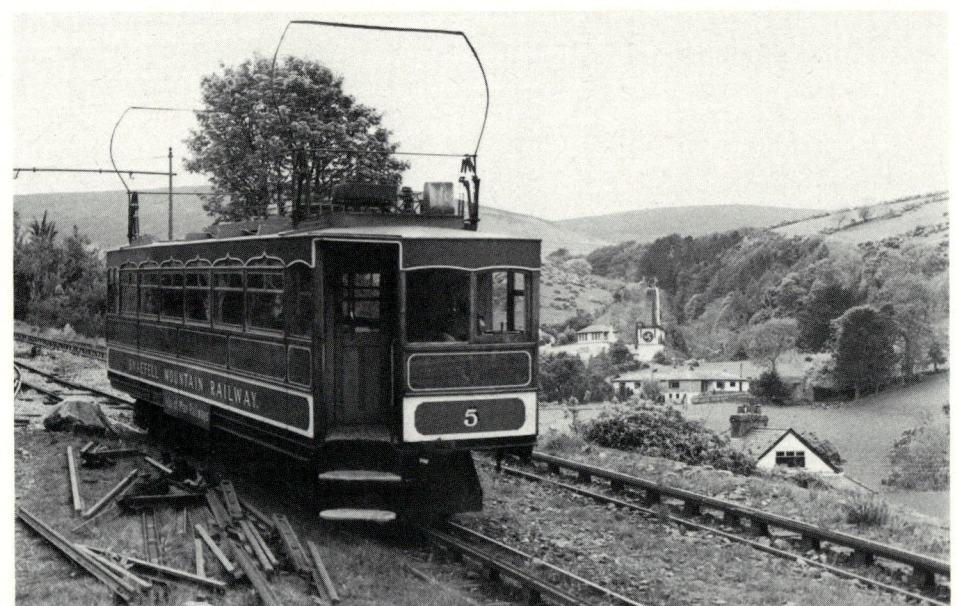

buying new was considered prohibitive so an unusual and original solution was implemented.

With London Transport employed both as consultants and contractors, seven disused cars were bought from Aachen, Germany. Six of them were taken to LT's Acton Works where the motors were fitted into new bogies; the wheelsets and Fell braking equipment were reused. All other useable equipment was removed from the cars and taken to Derby Castle; there the controllers and alarm gongs were fitted to the Snaefell cars. The Aachen resistors were roof-mounted and of insufficient capacity to allow continuous rheostatic braking on the downhill journey so additional resistances were installed later. The seventh car was shipped to Derby Castle and stripped for spares.

This modest modernisation programme has proved to be a great success; the cars are quieter, reliable, more efficient and less costly to run. The use of rheostatic braking is responsible for most savings, both in reducing power consumption and in reducing wear and tear of the Fell brakes. There can be few electric systems celebrating their 90th birthdays with their original cars having only had one change of motors.

BRITISH TRAMS & TRAMWAYS in the 1980s

Seaton Tramway

That there are trams in East Devon is known to few, yet here purpose-built tramcars carry holidaymakers along the banks of the River Axe on a route which first saw passengers in 1868. However this is not a remnant of some long forgotten tramway system, nor can it be considered a preserved or museum line. Like the cars, the tramway was purpose-built.

Below:
Seaton & District Electric Tramway.

Below right:
The style of Seaton No 2 is that of a Metropolitan Electric Tramway 'A' class car; it seats 36 and was built in 1964. Here – on 27 July 1984 – it is at the tramway's northern terminus of Colyton, which is still being developed. The station building is the most substantial relic of the former branch line to be seen. *Author*

The Seaton Tramway has its origins in a portable 15in gauge line which was taken to garden fetes during the years 1948/50. A public service was operated at St Leonards-on-Sea during 1951 and at Rhyl from 1952. Two cars were built for the portable line, styled on a Darwen 'streamliner' and a Blackpool 'Boat'. At Rhyl they were joined by a freelance design open-top double-decker and an open bogie toastrack. In 1954 a second 'Boat' and a Blackpool 'Balloon' were built, by which time the owners, Modern Electric Tramways Ltd, were planning to move to the south coast.

A site, which was eventually occupied by a tramway one-mile long, had been found in Eastbourne, a lease being obtained from the local authority. In view of the number of passengers expected it was decided to increase the gauge to 2ft. Of the 15in gauge stock four vehicles were regauged, the

second 'Boat' became a works car and then the mobile shop, and the toastrack, unsuitable for regauging, was dismantled.

Services started at Eastbourne in 1955 and the first tram built especially for the line followed a year later. This was an open-top double-decker, capable of carrying 40 passengers; like the 15in gauge open-top car, it was of a freelance design. A second, similar, car entered service in 1958. A workshop was opened in 1959, the first vehicle to emerge from it being a 20-seat 'Boat' in 1961. Another double-deck open-top car, seting 36, was built in 1963. In the same year the former 15in gauge cars were sold, one going to Scotland (and now in Merseyside) and three to the USA.

Additions were made to the fleet in 1966, a single-deck 20-seat saloon, and in 1968, a third open-top double-decker and a works car. The latter is explained by the local

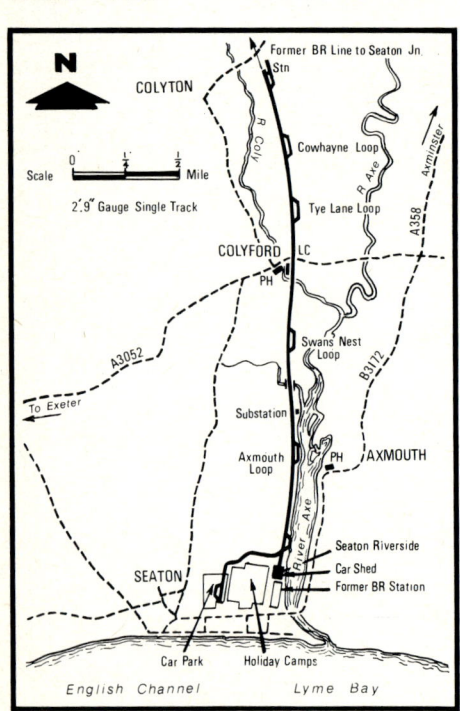

authority's unwillingness to give the company security of tenure; plans were being made for another move.

The company had been looking for an alternative site since 1964. Having decided that the uncertainties attached to being leaseholders could be avoided by becoming freeholders, it decided to seek out a former railway branch line trackbed which served a holiday resort, preferably on the south coast. Several were considered until 1966, when the Seaton branch was closed. The line, opened by the Seaton & Beer Railway Co in 1868, was a branch off the LSWR main line to Exeter and was built to carry holiday makers to the small resort of Seaton. The tramway company opened negotiations with British Rail and the local authorities and it was ultimately agreed that it should buy a three-mile section, from Colyton to the edge of Seaton. The mile of route from Colyton to Seaton Junction was not deemed to have any traffic potential and Seaton station was sold for industrial use. Agreement was also obtained for an extension from the trackbed to the central car park, giving better access to potential passengers.

The necessary Light Railway Orders

were obtained, which, strangely, did not include provision for the car park extension, and preparations were made for the move. The last services in Eastbourne ran in September 1969 and construction at Seaton started early the following year.

In planning for Seaton an early decision was taken to increase the track gauge again, to 2ft 9in. This was to allow for increased stability and higher speeds. A depot was built where the car park extension was to diverge from the trackbed and track laying commenced. By August 1970 it was possible to operate a service over nearly a mile of newly laid track; a temporary station was opened near the depot and power taken from batteries carried on a truck propelled by the service car. During the following winter tracklaying reached Colyford, just past the half way point. Overhead electric pickup was implemented in 1973, by which time two passing loops had been installed on the single line. The next task undertaken was the construction of the car park extension; it was opened in 1975. The last extension, to Colyton, was opened in 1980; there are two passing loops, plus a terminal loop, on this section. (There are also passing loops at Colyford and the depot and a terminal loop at Seaton).

The cars built at Eastbourne were constructed with the possibility of regauging the system in mind, so there were no difficulties, apart from shortage of time, in adapting the fleet to its new home. In the event the cars were regauged as labour permitted and traffic required. The mobile shop stayed on a 2ft gauge siding until the car park extension was opened, when it was given unpowered bogies of Seaton gauge; it is towed out to the car park each day the tramway operates. The Eastbourne-built single-deck saloon was modified by the addition of a top deck, entering service in this form in 1979. The works car was blown over in a gale in January 1980; it was rebuilt as a tower wagon the following year. In 1984 a new single-deck clerestory saloon entered service. Construction had actually started at Eastbourne but the car's origins were much older, having started life in London as Metropolitan Electric Tramways No 94 in

Above:
Cars Nos 2 and 12 inside the depot on 9 June 1974. No 12 was rebuilt to become a 52-seat open-top vehicle in 1979. At 31ft 6in long it is the longest of all the Seaton cars. Unlike the other double-deck cars its lower deck is totally enclosed. 27 July 1984. *Author*

Right:
In addition to being a crossing place for trams, Colyton is where the tramway crosses the road. Both users are protected by lights and bells. Car No 6 was built for the 2ft gauge Eastbourne Tramway. Styled on Bournemouth open cars it seats 40 and was built in 1956. A 27 July 1984 view. *Author*

Below right:
No 12 as built in 1966, when it was a 20-seat enclosed saloon car. 9 June 1974. *Ian Allan Library*

1906. In addition to its vintage body, it followed the manner of building the other cars, in using parts obtained from any number of previous operators, and not just from the United Kingdom, either. The 1984 car is smartly turned out in Metropolitan livery and lettered 'Seaton & District Tramway Company', the subsidiary of Modern Electric Tramways (note the similarity of initials with the MET!) which operates the tramway. The company also owns the bodies of two Bournemouth trams; they are stored for possible future use.

The company operates a daily service from Easter until the end of October. Its small permanent staff are supplemented by temporary personnel during the summer, when cars leave Seaton at 12min intervals. Since 1981 a limited winter service has been operated for the benefit of local inhabitants. Of particular interest is the unadvertised service operated, by arrangement, for birdwatchers. They find the quiet-running tramcars ideal for watching the inhabitants of the adjacent Axe estuary; these specials usually run during the dawn of summer weekends.

BRITISH TRAMS & TRAMWAYS in the 1980s

Great Orme Tramway

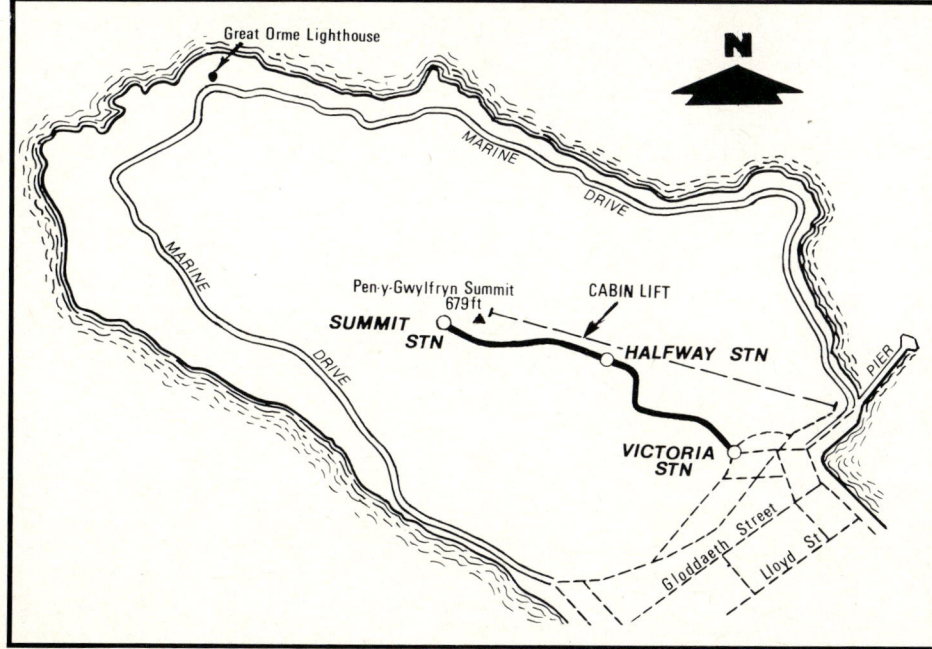

The North Wales town of Llandudno began to expand and develop as a seaside resort during the Victorian era. It was obvious that the large promontory which overlooked the town should feature in plans for its development. The headland, known as the Great Orme and offering fine views of Snowdonia and Anglesey, is 2½ miles long and half a mile wide; its summit is 679ft above sea level. The steepness of the lower reaches made the Great Orme a difficult or inaccessible place for the average Victorian holidaymaker to visit.

Ways of improving access were made from the 1880s onwards, but it was not until 1898 that powers were obtained for the construction of a tramway. It was to be built in two half-mile sections and the promoters were authorised to build a hotel at the summit, a prerequisite of all such schemes. The gauge was to be 3ft 6in, the same as the Snaefell Mountain Railway, but two more dissimilar lines could hardly be imagined! The Llandudno system was to be operated by cable haulage.

The contractors started work in 1901 and got the lower section ready for use the following year; the upper section was opened in 1903. Passengers flocked to the tramway as the promoters had anticipated; 77,410 were carried in 1903. Until 1907 profits were used to complete items of a capital nature; the lower terminal station built in 1904, for example; thereafter regular dividends were paid to shareholders.

As mentioned, the tramway was built in two sections. The lower section could be described as urban, running in the road or on a reservation alongside the road; the gradients are as steep as 1 in 4 and the cable

Above left:
Great Orme No 5 inside the lower station, called Victoria, on 13 July 1979. *M. F. Haddon*

Left:
The Great Orme Tramway.

runs in a duct under the track. The upper section is rural, running across open country where the steepest gradient is 1 in 10.3; railway type track is used here, and the cable runs on rollers between the rails. There is a passing loop on each section. The half way point is on a plateau, the site of the winding house and sheds for two cars. Passengers making the full journey have to walk, past these buildings, from one section to the other.

Four 48-seat cars were provided for the opening. Numbered 4-7 they remain in service today, Nos 4 and 5 on the lower section and 6 and 7 on the upper. As built, the windows were unglazed, a situation which was soon changed. The cars are fitted with an overhead pickup; it is not for power collection as many assume, but for communications with both the winding house attendant and the driver of the other car on the same section. The missing vehicle numbers were allocated to wagons.

A fatal accident in 1932 closed the tramway and, revealing defects in operation and management, forced the company into liquidation. The line was reopened in 1934 and in 1935 was sold to a syndicate which formed a company, Great Orme Railway Ltd, to operate it. The only outward change was the application of the new company's name to the cars.

In 1947 the Llandudno Urban District Council exercised its powers, contained in the 1898 Act, to purchase the undertaking. It took over on 1 January 1949. By this time more than 200,000 passengers were being carried each year. In 1957 the winding apparatus was converted from steam to electricity. Local government reorganisation saw the line transferred from the Llandudno UDC's transport department to Aberconwy Borough Council's tourism and amenities department. The new owner decided to commemorate the line's 75th anniversary by restyling the cars' paintwork and reverting to the tramway title.

Left:
Car No 6 in a cutting on the upper section in September 1983. *Author*

Below:
Lower section car No 4 at Half Way station. One of the competing aerial cars is seen on the right in this September 1983 photograph. *Author*

BRITISH TRAMS & TRAMWAYS in the 1980s

National Tramway Museum

The National Tramway Museum is the operating arm of the Tramway Museum Society. The Society was formed in 1955, establishing its museum site at Crich, Derbyshire in 1959 but the events which led to their creation actually commenced in 1948.

In that year members of the Light Railway Transport League, a society with an international membership whose primary objective was to promote tramways as a useful means of transport, organised a farewell tour of the Southampton tramway system. During the tour some of the participants decided to try to preserve one of the trams; they chose the diminutive 1903-built No 45 and succeeded in buying it for £10. They were then faced with the task of finding a home for it, not an easy matter; by 1960 the car had spent time at Leeds, Blackpool and Beaulieu, none of these locations proving ideal.

Meanwhile, the LRTL had, in 1949, formed a museums committee. Seven trams had been entrusted to it by 1951, although housing them was demonstrably impossible leading to the two from Liverpool being quickly scrapped because they had deteriorated beyond repair. There were also problems within the society, between members who wanted to demonstrate that tramways could be modernised and form the basis of transport systems of the future,

Left:
Southampton No 45, the first enthusiast preserved tram, the purchase of which eventually lead to the establishment of the museum at Crich. It was built in 1903 and extensively modified on three occasions. No 45 arrived at Crich in 1960. It is seen in the depot yard during 1984. *Author*

Below:
The National Tramway Museum, Crich.

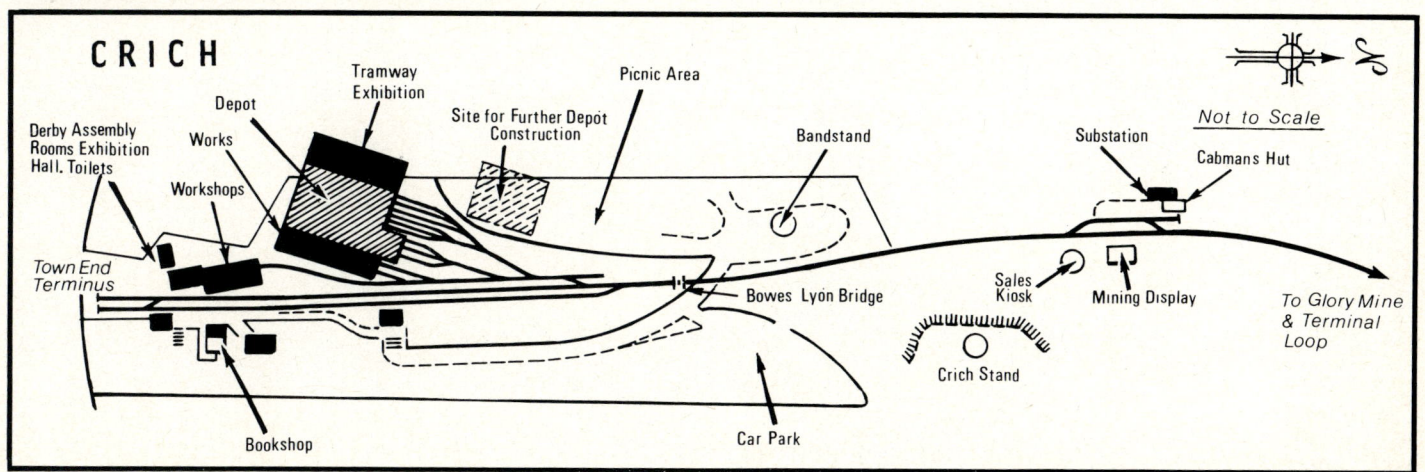

and those who wanted to demonstrate the past by preserving the most ancient cars they could find. In 1955 the unincorporated Tramway Museum Society was formed to take over the assets and responsibilities of the committee.

The new society continued the search for suitable premises in which to house the collection. In this its objectives were to find a site which was both accessible to members and sufficiently far from urban areas to deter visits from vandals. An early ambition was to demonstrate the trams in realistic surroundings, so land was also required for that. News of a suitable location was passed to the society in 1958.

The Talyllyn Railway had bought track materials from the then recently closed limestone quarry at Crich, eight miles from Matlock. The quarry had been opened by George Stephenson in 1840. A 3ft 3in gauge railway, 2.25 miles long, was built to carry the output to kilns adjacent to both the Cromford Canal and the North Midland Railway near Ambergate. The quarry and its railway were closed in 1957; the quarry was subsequently re-equipped and reopened, its product being carried away by road. The TR sent working parties to Crich to lift and load the track. Two working party members were also members of the TMS; they thought the site could meet the society's requirements and reported their observations to the relevant persons.

Following an inspection and an extraordinary general meeting of the society, the first tramcar arrived at Crich in May 1959; by the end of 1960 more than 20 were on site.

It was very nearly too late, but the closure of the last major tramway systems, at Leeds (1959), Sheffield (1960) and Glasgow (1962), provided a great deal of material, including cars, spares and equipment, for the new museum. A bonus was the four restored cars donated by Blackpool following their 75th anniversary procession.

The society had already realised that if it were to be successful it must have adequate buildings for its collection. The first of its depot buildings was erected in 1961, two years before it was able to offer (horse) tram rides to the public. To ensure that matters did not get out of hand and the site littered with rotting tram bodies, cars were only accepted as donations, and only then if the donor (or the sponsors of a vehicle) provided 50% of the cost of housing it. In this way accommodation for 40 cars has been built; an additional building, with room for 24 cars, is proposed.

The horse tram service commenced in 1963 was withdrawn the following year when Blackpool & Fleetwood No 2 inaugurated the electric service; the horse cars now emerge only on special occasions. The tramway at this point was very short – in 1966 it was extended so that it was about 400yd long.

Many of the trams collected when the museum first opened its doors came direct from service with their previous operator, as a result they were relatively modern. It was found to be possible to add to the collection by acquiring cars which had been disposed of many years previously, either when modernisation programmes were being implemented or when systems were

Right:
Early days. The first permanent depot to be built at Crich was erected in 1961. The three visible inhabitants are Southampton No 45; Sheffield No 510, built in 1950 and the last to run there; and Glasgow No 812, built in 1900 as an open-top car. The depot now has doors, lighting and a concrete floor. *Author's Collection*

Below:
The first passenger services at Crich were horse-drawn, using Sheffield horse car No 15. Chesterfield No 8 was loaned to the museum in 1982 after it had been restored by Chesterfield Transport; the car was built in 1899 and spent many years as a summer house after the Chesterfield system was electrified in 1904. *David Stuttard*

a New York car exported to Vienna as part of the postwar Marshall Aid Program. It arrived at Crich in 1970 and has been restored to New York condition, complete with 1940s period advertising.

The desire to show off the trams in a realistic setting began to gather momentum in 1967 when a report on the museum's development was published. The creation of a typical Edwardian street scene around the tramway terminus, called Town End, was envisaged. A cobbled roadway with gas lamps, enamelled adverts, a shop window, a pillar box, a police post (used by tramway operating inspectors), wrought iron railings and gates (the latter from Marylebone station), and a cast iron tram shelter are just a few of the many facets which have gone into developing the street. The structural focal point, however, is on a much larger scale than any of these, for in 1972 the facade of the Derby Assembly Rooms was removed to Crich for re-erection. It now hides an exhibition room, conveniences and the museum's library. Plans made to accommodate the facade from Derby's Midland Railway station, demolished

Below:
Some museum services were steam-hauled in 1966, using the Beyer Peacock tram engine. It was built in 1885 and exported to New South Wales. It was not a success and was returned to the builders who used it as a works shunter until 1959. It was stored by Beyer Peacock until it was donated to the museum in 1962. Following an extensive overhaul it is proposed to use the vertical boilered machine with the Dundee steam tram trailer currently being restored. On the left in this photograph is the Leeds tower wagon, built as a spare time project, using materials unwanted from other jobs, in 1932. It has been at Crich since 1969.   *Author*

Left:
The focal point of the museum's Town End townscape is undoubtedly the Derby Assembly rooms facade. Here it provides a backdrop for Leeds No 180, one of a hundred 60-seat cars built by Brush in 1931. It ran in the last tram procession in Leeds in 1959 and arrived at Crich in 1960. It re-entered museum service in 1982 after a heavy overhaul and is seen here during the summer of 1984.   *Author*

being abandoned. In the intervening years they had been used as chicken huts or holiday homes; they would require the expenditure of much effort and cash and painstaking restoration before they could make a public appearance again. Into this category came Leicester No 76. Sold in 1947 when the Leicester system was being run down prior to closure, it was taken to a farm near Goole. It arrived at Crich in 1960 and became the first major restoration project undertaken there. Working in very primitive conditions, both environmentally and regarding equipment, an immaculate restoration was completed in 1969, ironically the year that the museum's own workshop became available for use. It set an admirable precedent for future restorations.

To round out the tramcar picture, some vehicles were sought from abroad. To date the collection includes specimens from Portugal, Eire, South Africa, Czechoslovakia and Austria. The latter was

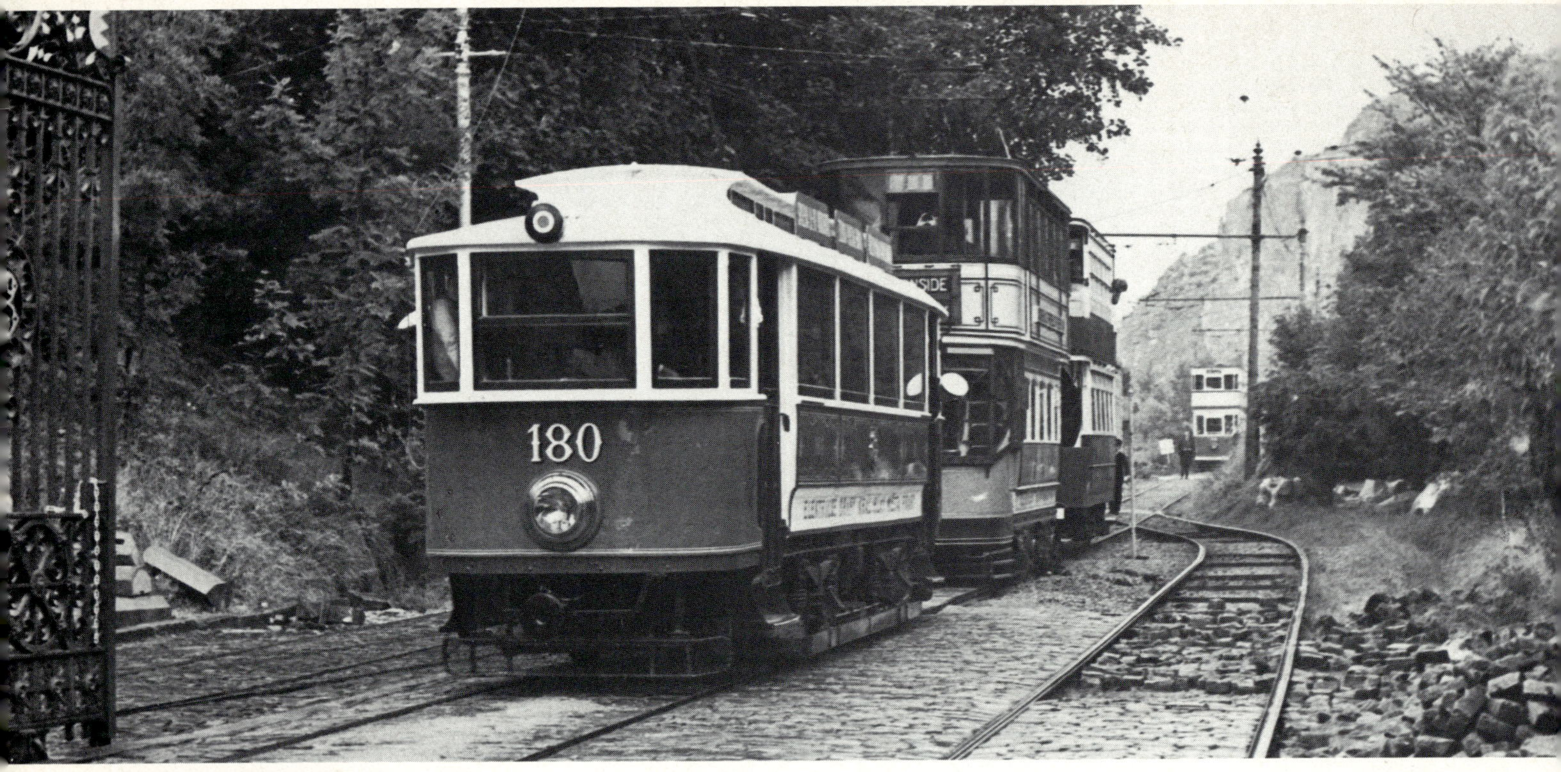
180

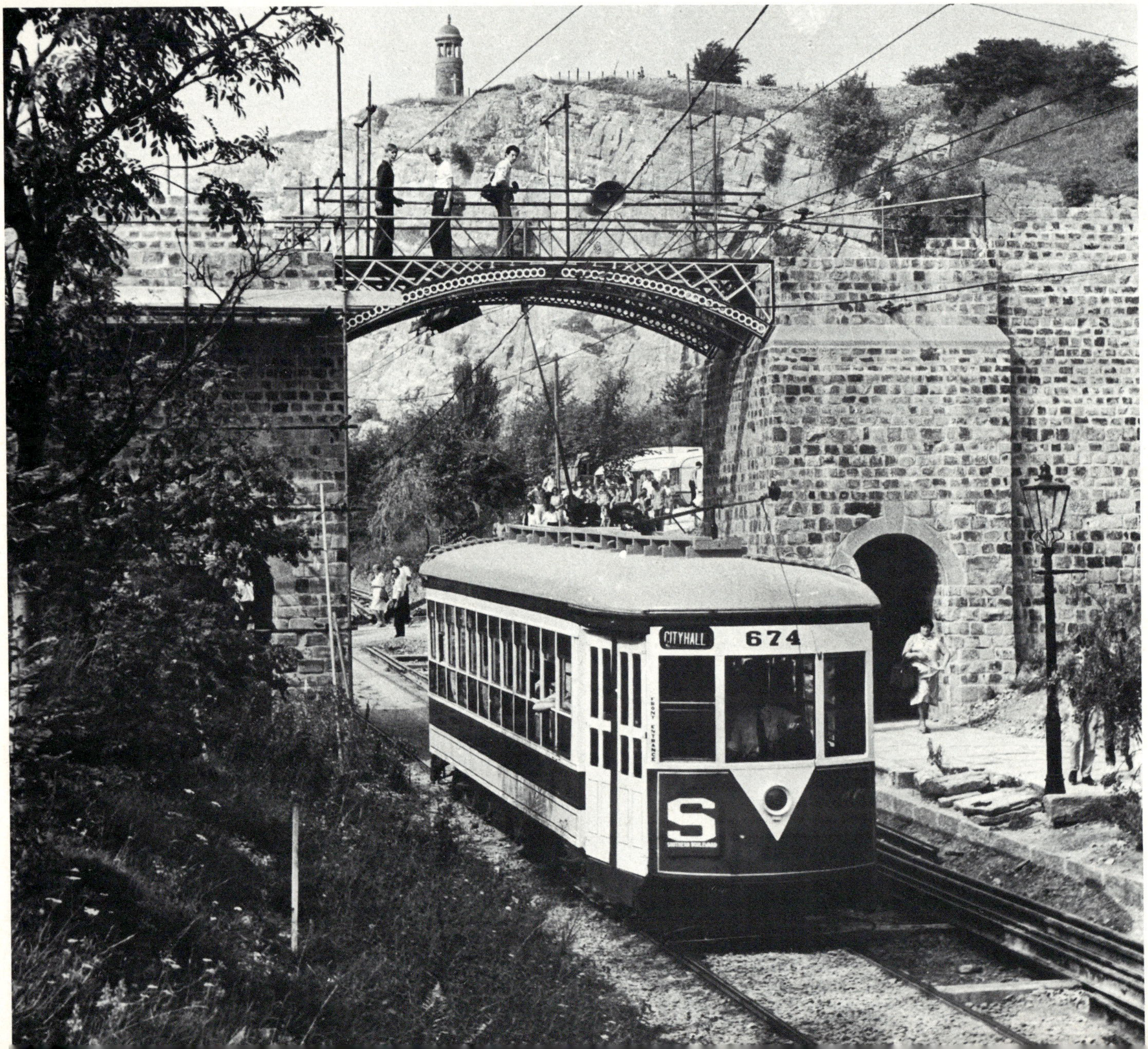
CITY HALL
674
S

Above left:
On 27 August 1984, a line-up of trams waiting to enter the single line to Wakebridge has another No 180 bringing up the rear. This one was built in Czechoslovakia for use in Prague in 1908. It was presented to the museum, in a restored condition, following a visit by a group of Czech tramway engineers in 1967. Shipment from Prague was implemented two days before the Russians invaded in 1968. *Author*

Left:
Car 674 was built in New York in 1939 and arrived at the museum, via Vienna, in 1970. It is seen on 27 August 1984 passing under the unfinished Bowes-Lyon bridge. Behind is Crich Stand, the Sherwood Foresters' war memorial. *Author*

Above:
Blackpool No 166 was one of six cars built at Rigby Road works in 1927. Consigned to storage as unserviceable in 1941 it was retrieved for use by television crews televising the illuminations in 1953. It was returned to store during the 1960s and given to the museum in 1972. It has been in service since 1974. The jazz band – seen on 27 August 1984 – is one of the features of the Grand Transport Extravaganza held annually at Crich since 1968. In addition to running as many trams as possible in an intensive service, attractions have included vintage road vehicles, flypasts, a flea market, a fairground and portable railways. *Author*

Right:
Blackpool No 40 on the same date as restored for its visit to its home town in 1985. In the background are tips of crushed stone awaiting removal for road building. *Author*

under a modernisation scheme regrettably came to naught. At the 'country' end of Town End the site is being enclosed by the erection of a 20ft span cast iron bridge. Built in 1844, it came from Stagenoe Park, Hertfordshire, home of the Bowes-Lyon family. Suitable buttresses of York and Derbyshire stone have been designed to carry the bridge, which will become the main pedestrian access from the car park.

The tramway was extended to

Wakebridge, half a mile from Town End, and now the half way point, in 1968. The area is riddled with old metal mines so a small mining exhibit has been established. The switchroom of the museum's substation is also open for public viewing here.

In 1978 the tramway was extended again, to Glory Mine, making the whole line just over a mile long. Construction had been undertaken using labour recruited under the terms of a job creation project; the society provided the materials, the government paying for the 17 personnel employed. Similar teams have been used for tramcar restoration and other projects, including the Bowes-Lyon bridge.

As with all the best museums it is not possible to display all the exhibits at once, so the surplus, or unrestored, are placed in store, in this case the former goods shed at Clay Cross. Some restoration work is also undertaken here. To ease the load on facilities at Crich, a number of trams have been restored elsewhere, by members or, at Bolton, at a workshop funded by the Manpower Services Commission. Outside work undertaken by TMS members has the benefit of involving those who could not otherwise participate in museum activities. An added attraction has been the incentive of working on vehicles from the volunteers' own locality, namely Liverpool, London and Manchester. The loan of cars to Blackpool has already been mentioned; other cars have been loaned, on a long term basis, to the Heaton Park project and to Hull Museums.

There are now over 50 vehicles, of all sorts, shapes and sizes, in the museum collection. Many of them are restored to an exhibition finish, and a good number of them are in working order. It is hardly surprising, therefore, that the museum has become a major tourist attraction and, for those devotees of street and railed transport, a centre of excellence. The adoption, in 1981, of the title 'National Tramway Museum' was only right and proper.

Above:
Museum visitor. Blackpool No 710 will return home one day. By the end of 1984 it had travelled 1,938 miles in museum service, a figure computed to be the equivalent of 88 trips to Fleetwood, on a line slightly over a mile long! The flagman is controlling the crossing to the Extravaganza flea market area seen on 27 August 1984. *Author*

Right:
On the extension to Glory Mine riders have an impressive view over the Derwent valley. LCC No 106 traverses this section on 1 July 1984. A 56-seat car, No 106, was built in 1903 without a trolley pole, for it was designed to operate on the conduit system. Later it was enclosed and a trolley fitted. In the 1920s it was extensively modified for use on snow clearing duties. It was kept when the London system closed and eventually a 12-year restoration was started, in London, in 1971. Upon completion No 106 was transferred to Crich where it was made operational within three months. *Author*

BRITISH TRAMS & TRAMWAYS in the 1980s

East Anglia Transport Museum

Founded in 1965, the East Anglia Transport Museum is situated on a three-acre site at Carlton Colville, near the seaside resort of Lowestoft in Suffolk. It is a museum run by enthusiasts dedicated to all forms of wheeled transport. On the site there is a narrow gauge railway, the makings of a 1930s period street wired for trolleybus operation and, of interest here, a tramway, part of which is incorporated into the street.

The motivation for building a tramway at the museum came right at the start, for those involved already owned three trams, from Lowestoft, Glasgow and London. The least travelled of these is also of local interest, being Lowestoft Corporation Tramways' No 14, built in 1904 as a 48-seat, open-top double-decker. Still in original condition when the 3ft 6in gauge Lowestoft system closed in 1931, it was sold for use as a summer house. Rescued for preservation in 1962, it now has a standard gauge truck, although it is the only car not to have run at the museum.

Glasgow 'Coronation' No 1245, an enclosed 64-seat double-deck car built in 1939 was purchased for preservation in 1962, when the Glasgow system closed. After standing in the open in Leicestershire for two years, it moved to Suffolk in 1964. Restored to working order, it ran at Carlton Colville for the first time in 1980.

London County Council No 1858 is another double-deck enclosed car, but with 74 seats, and was built in 1930. Bought privately in 1952, when the last of London's tramways were abandoned, it was displayed in the open at Chessington Zoo until it was

Right:
East Anglia Transport Museum, Carlton Colville.

Below:
A 1974 view of the East Anglia Transport Museum's street; the track layout has been changed subsequently. The service car is Blackpool 'Standard' No 159, once an illuminated car. *R. Makewell*

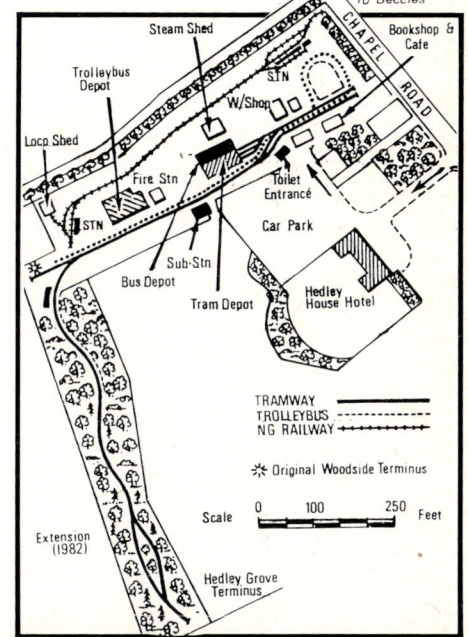

moved to Suffolk in 1964. It has run at the museum on special occasions. An extensive overhaul should be completed by 1986.

Minimal track laying was carried out until the depot had been built in 1966/7. It was 1972 before the museum was sufficiently developed to allow regular public admission. By this time the tramway was 200yd long and there were two more trams in the collection, both from Blackpool. First to arrive, in 1967, was No 159 – the last of the illuminated 'Stndards'. It is of 1927 vintage, an enclosed double-decker with seating for 78, the largest in the museum. All the exterior lighting has been removed and the car is in regular service. The other Blackpool car is No 11, a 'Railcoach' style 'Sun Saloon' built in 1939 and modified in 1952 for regular service on the Marton route. It was withdrawn in 1965, having been in store for the previous three years, and reached Carlton Colville, via the abortive scheme to restore the Hayling Island branch as a tramway, in 1967. It is in regular museum service.

In 1982 a 200yd extension was opened into adjacent woodland, the new terminal being called Hedley Grove. Construction work had been carried out over the previous 18 months. The new line was inaugurated by Blackpool No 159, an apt choice as this car had run the first trials on the original tramway in 1970. Just before the extension was opened, the tram collection had been increased by the addition of No 474 from Amsterdam. This car had been built as a tram trailer in 1929, motorised in 1938 and allocated to the tram driving school in 1972. Still in working order, with only 20 seats it is the smallest car at the museum.

The body of a London trailer was moved to the museum from a farm near Sevenoaks in 1985.

BRITISH TRAMS & TRAMWAYS in the 1980s

Black Country Museum

At the Black Country Museum the tramway has been provided to transport visitors across the 26-acre site. After several years' preparation and three years of on-site development the museum was opened in 1979. It is situated in Dudley, north of Birmingham, on land adjacent to a basin on the Dudley Canal. Formed under the auspices of the Dudley Metropolitan Borough Council, it has been in the care of the Black Country Museum Trust since 1975.

The objectives of the museum are to illustrate the way of life of the Black Country people, where they lived, how they worked and how the area became the centre of industrial Britain. To this end a village has been developed around the canal basin, including houses, shops, small factories, a pub and a chapel; all these buildings have been removed from other sites in the locality where several had been threatened with demolition. A coal mine exhibit has

Above:
Dudley & Stourbridge No 5 is the only tram to run at the Black Country Museum so far. The body of a similar vehicle is used as a waiting shelter. A summer 1983 view. *Author*

Right:
Kept in the depot at Dudley is a Birmingham Central Tramways car of 1888. Built to operate on a route where the cars were cable-hauled, it remained in service until 1911. Not obvious from the photograph is the fact that it is a double-deck car. *Author*

Left:
Black Country Museum, Dudley.

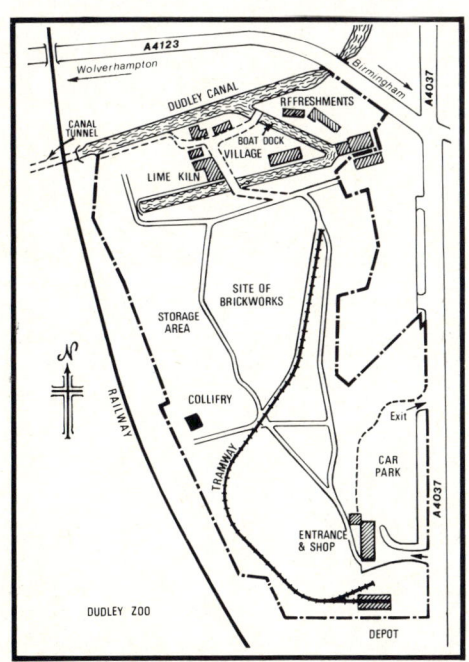

been built on the top of an abandoned shaft found on the site. A brickworks is one of the items proposed for future construction. Transport is demonstrated by the canal and the tramway; a trolleybus circuit is also proposed.

The tramway was built with the aid of a grant from the West Midlands County Council. The local gauge of 3ft 6in has been adopted; the line is 525yd long and opened in 1980. It starts at the depot, near the main entrance, and runs to a terminus just outside the village. The only tram to operate here so far is Dudley, Stourbridge & District Electric Traction Company No 5 of 1920. The 32-seat enclosed saloon body has been restored with a regauged standard gauge truck from Belgium. Further tram bodies with local connections are stored for future restoration.

BRITISH TRAMS & TRAMWAYS in the 1980s

Heaton Park Tramway

Heaton Park, at over 600 acres the largest in Manchester, has been in public ownership since 1902. It is very popular with Mancunians and many facilities and attractions are provided for their use and entertainment. The first tramway which served the park was opened in 1903. By 1905 weekend traffic generated by the park was so great that a 400yd branch was laid into it, a waiting shelter for 2,000 being provided at the terminus a year later. The services which entered the park were as successful as anticipated but changing circumstances were to bring about the abandonment of the branch in 1934. A siding and the electrical equipment were removed, leaving only the twin tracks which were covered in tarmac and used for car parking.

The revival of the Heaton Park Tramway commenced in the 1960s, following the rescue of Manchester No 765, a single-deck combination (part open, for smokers, part enclosed) car, from a farm near Huddersield. After three years at Crich it was removed to Manchester for restoration by local enthusiasts. They looked for a local site on which to run their tram when the restoration was complete, proposing in 1967 a new line of tramway in Heaton Park to the City Council. This was turned down but the council did express an interest in supporting a tramway in the park if the costs were lower. A scheme involving the original park tramway, and converting the shelter into a depot, was then accepted for implementation when finances permitted.

Construction work started in 1977 when the council was able to take advantage of a

Above right:
Blackpool & Fleetwood No 40 undergoing restoration, now completed, in the Heaton Park depot on 7 April 1980. Part of the depot is given over to a display relating to Manchester's trams. *M. F. Haddon*

Right:
Heaton Park Tramway, Manchester.

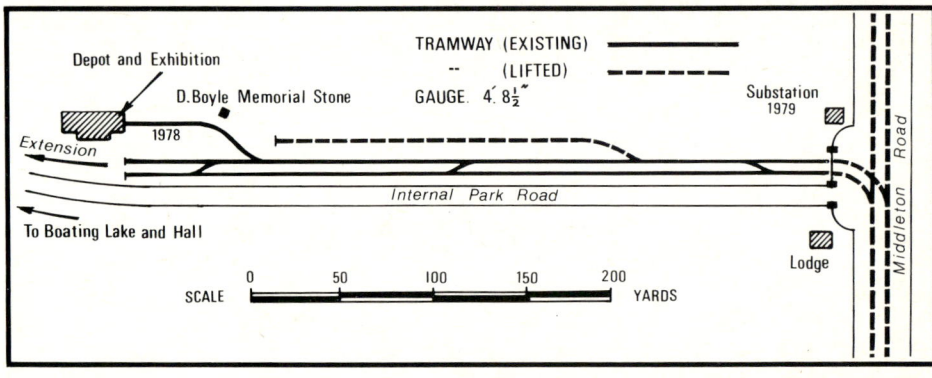

40

Above:
The beautifully restored Manchester No 765 by the Middleton Road gates terminus on 7 April 1980. Mancunians knew this class of tram as 'California' cars. *M. F. Haddon*

government-sponsored unemployment relief programme. The track was uncovered, a siding laid to the new depot, traction poles and cable erected, the substation built and equipped, the shelter's floor was excavated (to create sufficient headroom for the trams) and the shelter itself was enclosed. Work was completed in time for trial running to take place in 1979, the official opening following in 1980.

In the meantime the restoration of No 765 had been completed, the car having spent 1977/8 working at Crich. To provide a back-up, Blackpool & Fleetwood No 40 has been loaned from Crich. Another Manchester car, a four-wheel open top vehicle, is being restored for services in the park. No 765 was chosen to participate in the Blackpool celebrations; whilst it was away it was replaced by Blackpool 'boat' No 600 carrying its original number, 225.

As with the other attractions in the park, which include a model boating pool, a golf course, bowling greens, tennis courts and a pets corner, the tramway has proved to be very popular with visitors, despite being somewhat remote from the main thoroughfares. With this in mind work began on a 750yd extension to the boating lake in 1984, a move which will bring the trams to a larger audience. To operate the longer line a larger working fleet will be required so the works will include the building of a second depot. It was expected that part of the new line would be opened during 1985.

BRITISH TRAMS & TRAMWAYS in the 1980s

North of England Open Air Museum

'The great Northern experiencer' is how the North of England Open Air Museum describes itself, yet more accurately it is concerned with life in the northeast, encompassing the counties of Cleveland, Durham, Northumberland and Tyne & Wear. Based at Beamish Hall, near Gateshead, in County Durham, the museum has a railway (with the emphasis on goods and freight, rather than passengers), town, colliery and farm areas. All the buildings are reconstructions of typical structures threatened with demolition within the region covered. A standard gauge tramway, slightly over half a mile long, has been incorporated into the street scene; an attraction in its own right, it also serves to transport visitors about the site. It was opened in 1973. In addition to the town the tramway serves Foulbridge, home of some of the museum's other transport exhibits and the tram depot. The line is to be extended to pass the colliery site, terminating at the proposed new museum entrance and doubling its length.

It has not been possible for the museum to operate its tramway solely with trams of local origin, which has an unfortunate effect on authenticity. However the cars at the museum do form an interesting collection which is worth seeing.

The first tram to run at Beamish *is* of local origin, being built in Gateshead, for use in that town, in 1925. It is No 10, an enclosed single-deck saloon with 48 seats. When the Gateshead system closed in 1951 it was bought by British Railways for use on the Grimsby & Immingham Light Railway; it remained there until 1961 when that line closed. No 10 was then put into store until a home could be found for it. A claim made on behalf of Beamish was successful in 1968; restoration to Gateshead condition was complete in 1973, enabling the car to inaugurate the Beamish tramway.

The second car to run at Beamish is Sheffield No 342 which is in Gateshead livery. Built in 1907 as a 59-seat open-top double-deck vehicle it was rebuilt and enclosed in 1937. Upon withdrawal in 1956 it was put on show at the Clapham Museum of Transport. By the time it arrived at Beamish in 1973 the roof had been damaged so it has been restored to open-top condition. It has been in regular museum service since 1975.

Another Sheffield car, No 513, provides a striking contrast with No 342, for it was built as recently as 1950 and is a massive 62-seat double-decker. Withdrawn after only 10 years service it was purchased for private

Below:
North of England Open Air Museum, Beamish.

Below right:
Beamish street scene. Sheffield No 342 in 'Beamish' condition; the car was built with a roof, which may be restored when time and finances permit, and never carried the Gateshead livery in service. The street has been extended to the right since this picture was taken on 2 September 1984. *Author*

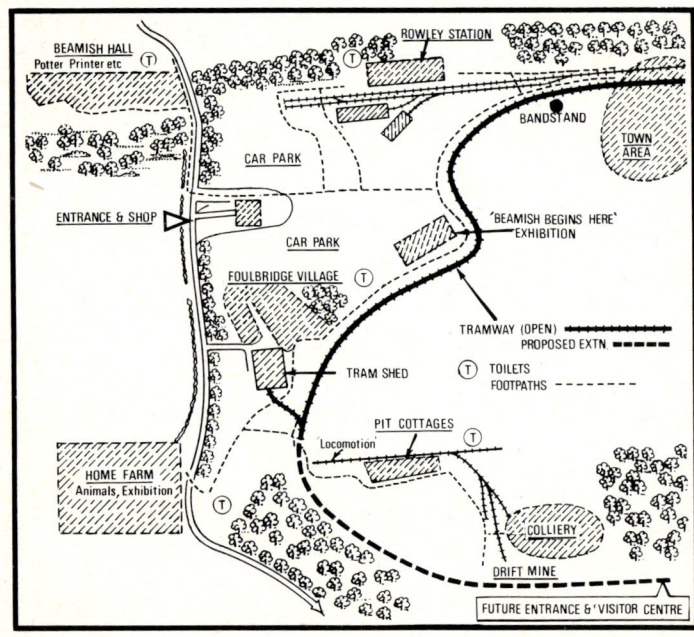

preservation; having difficulty in housing it, the owner gave it to the York Castle Museum in 1973. Displaying it proved to be impossible so No 513 was put into store. It moved to Beamish three years later entering service in 1983. It participated in the Blackpool centenary celebrations during 1985.

Ironically Beamish's most recent acquisition has come from Blackpool, being the overhead line car No 754. It is to be restored to passenger duties as an open-top car.

Above:
Gateshead No 10 before it moved to Beamish. It is seen in August 1967 at the British Transport Commission's Clay Cross store when it carried the livery of Grimsby & Immingham Light Railway No 26. Notice the BR crest on the side. *M. F. Haddon*

Right:
Sheffield No 513 is the third operational car at Beamish. From 1970 to 1973 it was stored at Oxenhope on the Keighley & Worth Valley Railway. It has been restored without the 'last tram' motifs, which have been retained on the similar No 510 at Crich. Photograph taken at Oxenhope, 12 September 1971. *M. F. Haddon*

Below:
Gateshead No 10 photographed on 20 June 1976 at the original Beamish tram terminus, near the rebuilt Rowley station. *M. F. Haddon*

BRITISH TRAMS & TRAMWAYS in the 1980s

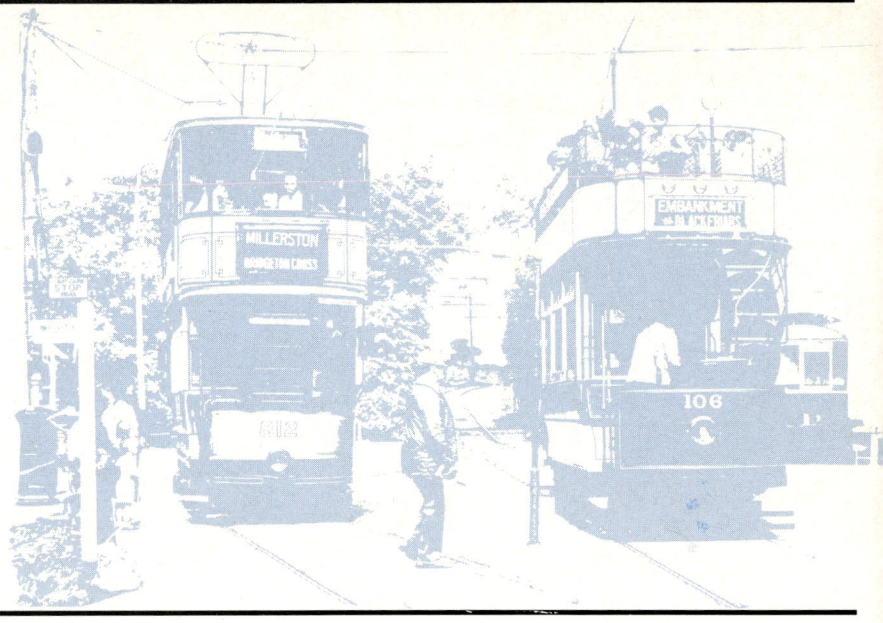

Museum Miscellany

In addition to the trams based on operating tramways already described, there are many kept in static conditions on sites all over the country. Some are being collected for use on proposed demonstration lines and may not yet be on public display. Possible operational projects have been announced for Bournemouth, 3ft 6in gauge electric; Low Moor, Bradford, standard gauge electric; Leicester, metre gauge electric; and Tyseley, West Midlands, standard gauge horse-drawn. At some museums there is little likelihood of their trams running again: Birmingham; Alford, Grampian; Cardiff and London are just a few of the locations which come to mind. One thing that is for sure, though: nothing should be taken for granted as far as trams are concerned; as the demand for working cars for new lines increases anything could happen. There are too many museums and vehicles to list here but a few of these miscellaneous cars are illustrated.

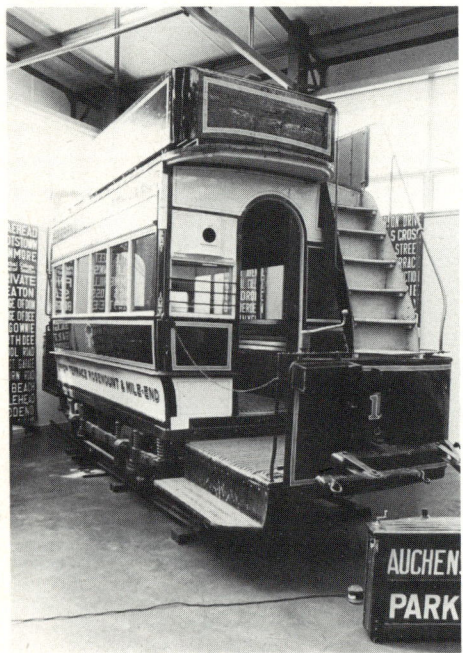

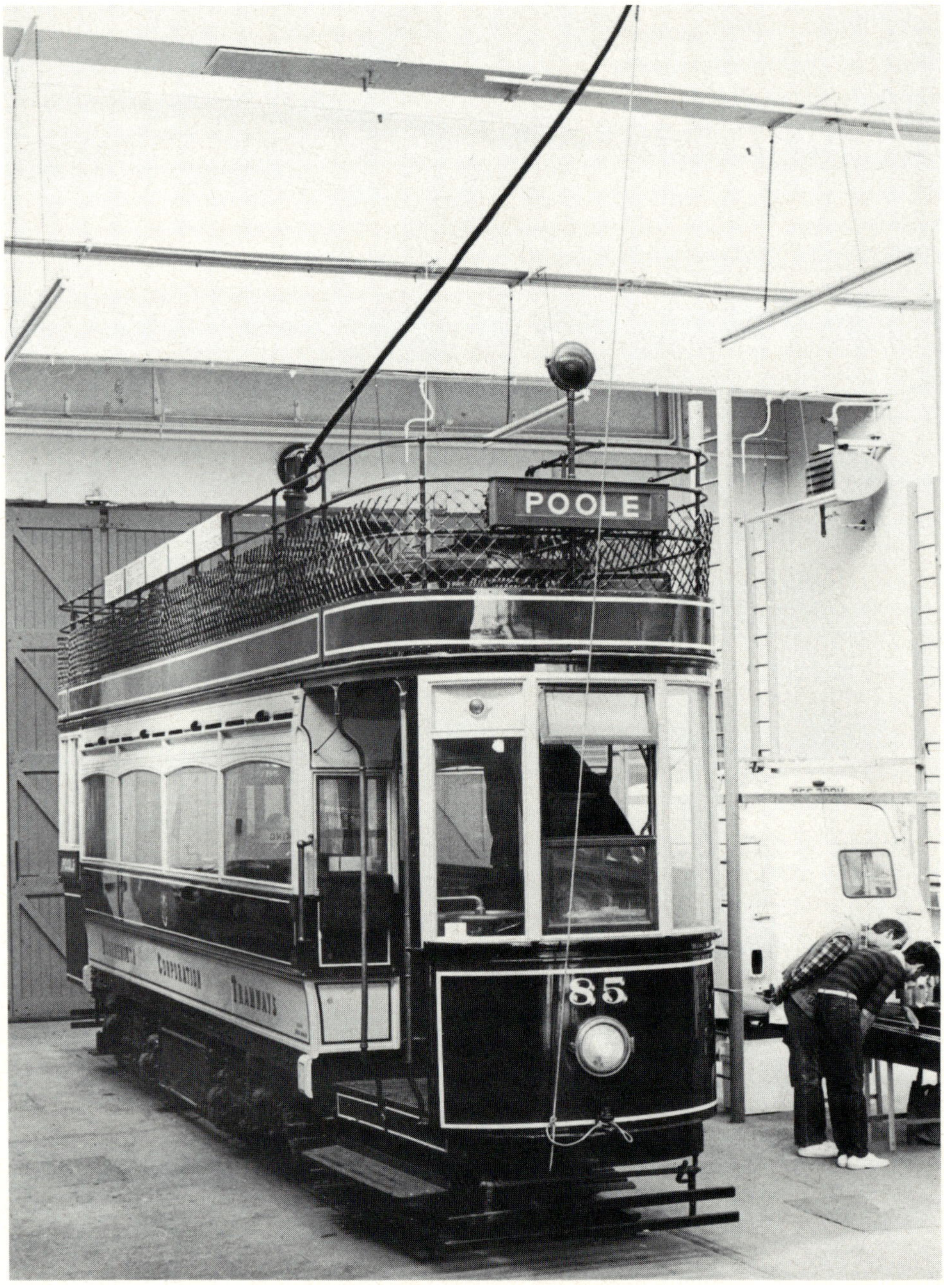

Far left:
Aberdeen No 1 is displayed at the Grampian Transport Museum at Alford. It was built as a horse car in 1896 and later electrified. It was reconverted for ceremonial use in 1924 and so survived. From 1963 to 1979 it was displayed in Edinburgh; it has been at Alford since 1982. *M. F. Haddon*

Left:
Bournemouth No 85 is a 68-seat car built in 1914 — seen here on 1 July 1984. It was sold to the Llandudno & Colwyn Bay Electric Railway Co when the Bournemouth system was abandoned in 1936. When the Llandudno system closed in 1956 No 85 was bought for preservation and later put on show at Clapham. It was moved to Bournemouth in 1974 and restored to original condition by 1977. This is one of a small collection of trams being stored for use on a proposed museum tramway in Bournemouth. During the summer months the public is admitted to the store on certain days when guided tours are given. *M. F. Haddon*

Above:
The Bradford Industrial Museum is home to Bradford No 104. Built in 1925, it was the official last tram when the system closed in 1950. It then spent three years as a scorer's box at a rugby ground before being returned to Bradford's Thornbury works by two enthusiasts. They obtained the parts missing which enabled restoration to early 1940s condition, and working order, to take place. It has been at the museum since 1975 and is seen here on 22 July 1984. *Author*

Top right:
The creation of the West Yorkshire Transport Museum at Low Moor has already been mentioned. Trams for this project are kept at the former Ludlam Street bus garage in Bradford. An inaugural open day was held here on 7 October 1984 when Blackpool 'Coronation' No 663 and Rotterdam No 109 were photographed. The museum also owns a second Rotterdam car, a Rotterdam trailer and two Blackpool trailers, Nos 689/90. The latter were acquired from GEC Traction who had been using them for traction experiments. *Author*

Above right:
This unrestored London double-deck horse tram is to be seen at the Caister Castle Motor Museum; 25 June 1982. *M. F. Haddon*

Right:
The Manchester, Bury, Oldham & Rochdale Steam Tramway Co Ltd's title is self explanatory. One of its tram engines, No 84, built by Beyer Peacock in 1886, has survived, last used as a works shunter by the Ince Forge Co in Wigan in 1952. Shown there on 18 April 1964 when stored at Crewe works, No 84 is now at the Dinting Railway Centre. *M. F. Haddon*

Top:
The London Transport Museum at Covent Garden contains three electric trams and an unrestored horse tram. Seen here on 30 April 1984, No 355 is the most modern, being built in 1931. It was sold to Leeds in 1950, returning to London for preservation when that system closed in 1959. *Author*

Top right:
Portsmouth No 84 was kept as a relic when Portsmouth abandoned its trams in 1936. It is a 46-seat car built in 1891 for the North Metropolitan Tramways Company, a concern which operated horse drawn trams in London. It was sold to the Provincial Tramways Company in Portsmouth in 1896 and became a member of the corporation's fleet in 1901; it was electrified two years later. It was photographed at the North End bus depot on 14 May 1976. *M. F. Haddon*

Above:
One of a host of interesting items to be seen at the Blists Hill Open Air Museum, Ironbridge, is this old tram body which had been used as a chapel. A 23 May 1976 photograph. *M. F. Haddon*

Right:
Glasgow No 585 has been the Science Museum's representative of a typical British tramcar since 1962. It was built in 1901 and progressively modernised over the years, although keeping many original features. Seven more Glasgow cars are kept in the Glasgow Transport Museum. *B. Walker*

Above:
The remains of Swindon No 13, shown here on 18 June 1984, were rescued from a farm in 1983. They are now at the Blunsdon depot of the Swindon & Cricklade Railway Society. The double-deck car was built in 1921. *M. F. Haddon*

Left:
Leicester City Council gave its German twin city, Krefeld, an unwanted double-decker bus. In exchange Krefeld gave Leicester a bus, a tramcar and trailer and sufficient electrical equipment to power a demonstration line! As yet nothing has come of any of the proposals to build a demonstration tramway so the cars are kept in the bus garage. The picture shows trailer No 41, built in 1956, and motor car No 412, built in 1957; they have been in Leicester since 1981. *Author*

Below left:
In addition to many locomotives and items of railway rolling stock Steamport, Southport has a small non-operational tram fleet. Stockport No 5 is being restored for use on the Heaton Park Tramway. Built in 1901 as a 56-seat, open-top, double deck car, the lower deck of No 5 spent 21 years as a summer house before being acquired for preservation; seen on 18 September 1982. *M. F. Haddon*

Below:
Two horse cars from the Leamington & Warwick system recently came to light and were moved to the Birmingham Railway Museum at Tyseley in the summer of 1984. Last carrying passengers in 1902, one had served as a bungalow extension, the other as a garden shed. They are virtually complete so the museum intends to restore them and operate a demonstration horse tramway; they are seen here on 17 August 1984. *Author*

Above:
The 18in gauge Highfield Electric Tramway is operated on the premises of the Whitchurch & District Model Engineering Society in Cardiff as seen on 17 September 1977. *M. F. Haddon*

Above right:
Some tramcars find new uses outside museums and preservation. This Pwllheli & Llanbedrog horse car was rescued from a farm and is now to be found outside the station at Pwllheli — where it was photographed on 3 May 1983 — in use as a taxi drivers' office. *Author*

Right:
There are still some major tramway artefacts to be found, scattered about the country as can be seen in this 30 April 1984 view. The Kingsway tram subway was opened from Southampton Row to Aldwych in 1906, a southern extension to the Embankment following two years later. The subway was enlarged to take double-deck cars in 1930, reopening in 1931. Closure was to come in 1952, following which it was used to store buses for a time. In 1964 the section from the Embankment to the Kemble street corner of the Kingsway was re-opened as an underpass for light vehicles. Part of the remainder has become the Greater London Council's Emergency Co-ordination Centre. The northern entrance remains unaltered, complete with tracks and conduit, only a short distance from the London Transport Museum. *Author*

Below right:
Tramway or railway? Scottish Agricultural Industries operates this line in Chapel Street, Aberdeen; it runs between the SAI factory and BR's Waterloo goods depot. The small Ruston diesel is struggling with a tanker of anhydrous ammonia on 15 August 1979. *R. E. Ruffell*

Below:
Many of the trams illustrated here in ths August 1983 photograph have been retrieved from secondary usage but there could be as many waiting to be found. Leicester No 59 is still mouldering away on a Leicestershire farm, almost consumed by the boscage. The top deck of No 31, alongside and behind No 59, has already collapsed into itself. Parts from these cars were taken for the restoration of No 76 at Crich. *Author*